P9-DSX-626

GROWING UP
SHAKER

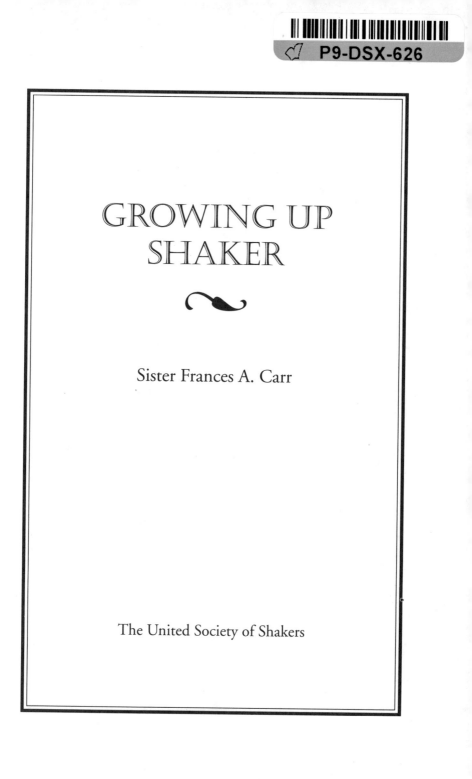

Sister Frances A. Carr

The United Society of Shakers

Copyright © 1995 by The United Society of Shakers

All rights reserved

Printed and bound in the United States of America

Third Printing

For Sister Mildred who made
"Growing Up Shaker"
a special experience for so many

Acknowledgments

Special thanks to my brother Bill for jogging my memory. I also offer my thanks to Anne Gilbert for her editorial assistance and to Brother Arnold for all of his help.

Foreword

In our country today, we have Aid to Dependent Children and Social Security which enable parents to keep their families together during difficult times. In years past, these programs did not exist, but one option people had was to take their children to live with the Shakers.

Children from broken homes and orphanages came to Shaker Communities in larger numbers after the Civil War. Widows or widowers with children found a refuge with the Shakers. Some parents indentured their children to the Shakers. Others would bring their children when they were unable to cope, and come for their children when their lives improved. This charitable work of the Shakers was a service to the towns, counties, and states.

Those who placed children with the Shakers, knew these children would be fed, clothed, and cared for in a loving way. They knew their children would receive a good upbringing, a good education and learn skills and trades.

The Sabbathday Lake Shaker Community took children in until the 1960's. At that time, because of the size of the Community, the members did not feel they were able to provide the day-to-day care needed by children. The State laws had also changed, and children were placed in nuclear homes rather than in religious communities.

Chapter One

❧ ❧ ❧

I Come to the Shakers

As I awoke, a strange noise came into my half-conscious state again. It was not like the noises of the city, even a small city. I opened my eyes and looked around and realized that of course I would hear strange sounds. I was in a strange place. The night before I had arrived at Shaker Village with my little sister, Ruth.

I looked for Ruth and saw her sleeping peacefully with just the top of her black head showing. In spite of the heat of the early August morning, little Ruth was wrapped tightly in her bedding. My big sister Katie was looking at Ruth. Katie had come to the Shakers earlier, and we were now joining her. Katie started to laugh, "I guess you never heard a rooster before." I didn't answer. I was afraid of seeming stupid, but I never had heard a rooster before.

I got up and dressed while most of the other girls in the room were still sleeping. The room was large with six small beds in it. Each bed had a chair beside it, and there was a marble sink in the corner of the room. A large part of one wall had a row of drawers which I would later learn was called a built-in cupboard and drawers. There was also a second door, which I discovered later opened into the room where Sister Mary Beckwith, the caretaker, slept.

I started out of the room, planning to go downstairs and out of doors, when another girl woke up and said, "You're not supposed to go out unless Sister Mary says you can."

"I was only going as far as the porch," I replied defiantly. I went downstairs, opened the door, and went out on the huge porch. I looked across the fields to where a cluster of buildings stood. One huge red building was high above the others which appeared to be little more than unpainted shacks. Large stacks of lumber were in the area of the buildings. I decided I must be looking at the lumber mill. It smelled delightful, like the sun baking the boards. While I was looking around, I noticed a play house and set of swings close to the porch. Before I could make up my mind to go and try the swings, I was startled by the sound of a loud bell ringing.

Group of children photographed at the Children's House. I am the girl at the extreme left. This picture was taken shortly after my arrival.

I rushed back into the house, thinking that now Ruth would be awake and looking for me. When I got to our room, Ruth was already up and talking with Sister Mary, who was helping her choose a dress to wear. I quickly stepped up and told Ruth that it was going to be very hot, and she should wear a dress with shorter sleeves. Sister Mary looked right at me and said, "I am taking care of Ruth, and I will tell her what dress to wear."

I replied, "I am her sister, and I promised that I would take care of her."

At this, Sister Mary said, "The bell has rung, and if we do not go, we will be late for breakfast. We can talk later. For now, I will say that your little sister needs a mother, and I will be that mother." It was then that I realized that I would not have an easy time dealing with Sister Mary.

I followed the other girls. There were ten of them, ranging in age from little girls even younger than Ruth to three teenagers about Katie's age. We walked to the huge brick house which was across the walk from the Children's House.

As we entered the brick house, people were coming from every direction. They all seemed to be going into a small room, called the waiting room, where they sat on long benches. I started to follow Katie into the room, when Sister Mary took my hand and said, "Oh, nay, you come with me. I like to keep the little ones with me where I can keep track of them."

I wanted to say, "I am not a little one. I am ten years old, and I have been helping to care for my little sister and doing all sorts of errands for a long time." But I thought I had upset Sister Mary enough already, and I went with the other little girls into the huge dining room.

There were six long tables and one small one set up for breakfast. As soon as we got to the small table, which was the children's table, a buzzer sounded. A parade of people began coming in from two doors. The first one in was a tiny little old lady who was wearing a dress which came down to her shoes. The shoes barely showed beneath her dress. She was also wearing a little lace cap on her head. I soon discovered that this was Eldress Prudence Stickney. Eldress Prudence was followed by several other older ladies who also wore long dresses and caps. After them came a number of younger ladies with shorter dresses and no caps. Behind them were the older girls from the Children's House who had been allowed to sit in the waiting room.

I had been so busy watching the women and children march in that I did not realize that there were a few boys and a couple of older men. Later I learned that the men were Brothers. The boys lived at the Trustees' House under the care of Sister Jennie Mathers. When everyone was in the dining room and every place was filled, the whole gathering knelt behind their chairs. They stayed in this position until the little lady who had been first to march in said, "Amen."

Even though there was apple pie for breakfast, I was not very hungry. There was also hot oatmeal, toast, applesauce, and huge pitchers of milk. When I looked at Ruth, who was seated next to me, I noticed that she had started to cry. This was probably because everything was so strange. She was homesick and a little frightened with so many people looking at her. Whenever a new girl came to Shaker Village, there was always a lot of interest in her on the part of the rest of the Community. Sister Mary told us that no one talked at the table. All I could hear was the sound of dishes and silverware, and a cough now and then. Once the hot oatmeal was served, Ruth forgot her anxiety and ate in great style. After a few days at the Community, Ruth became known as the one who would clean up her older sister's plate. This was lucky for me as long as we sat next to each other and were fast enough to switch plates. But this luck would not last once I was moved to the table where the older girls were.

Once breakfast was over, we all returned to the Girls' House with Sister Mary. The Children's House was charming in many ways. The daily life took place on the first floor. A huge room took up the entire south side of the house. One half of this room was where Sister Mary and her assistant worked, and the other half was for the children. The room had seven windows so it was always light and airy. On the children's side was a low bench-like table which went the full length of the east side of the room. This was for the little girls to sit at and draw, write, or whatever. There was a built-in cupboard with ten drawers. Each little girl used a drawer in which she kept her personal belongings, books, and sewing items.

Children's House. Built in 1796 and remodeled in 1901.

During the 1920's, Elder William Dumont made chairs for the girls living in the Children's House. Each little chair had the name of a girl on the front of it. By the time I came, Elder William was no longer alive, but the chairs he made were still in the Children's House. There were other small-sized chairs in the room, including a couple of rocking chairs. A wood stove dominated much of the space that separated the children's side from the caretaker's side. Sister Mary and her assistant both had Shaker sewing desks made by Elder Henry Green who was famous for his woodwork. They also had Shaker rocking chairs and straight-backed Shaker chairs with taped seats.

Across the hall from the work and play room was the good room. This was used only on Sundays or for special occasions. I would go to Sunday School here. Classes were held for both the younger children and the teenagers. Sister Mary taught the younger children on Sunday afternoon, and Sister Della Haskell taught the teen class an hour later. Sister Della had moved to Sabbathday Lake when the Alfred Shaker Community merged with Sabbathday Lake in 1931.

The good room was different from other rooms in the house. Besides having a piano, it had stuffed chairs and a small black sofa made of horsehair. The sofa was shiny but itchy to sit on. A large closet in the room contained the Children's Library. I was delighted to find such books as the entire collection of Little Prudie, a collection of Nancy Drew, and many others with appealing titles. Before coming to the Shakers, I had had my own library card at the Lewiston Public Library and had read one or two of the Nancy Drew books.

As I came into the house, I noticed a large room across the hall. This was where Sister Susie lived with her sister, a nurse. Sister Susie was an invalid, and her sister came to care for her for a while. A small woodshed opened into the hall, and in this room were a few rabbits which were pets for the children. In the cellar was a huge wood furnace, and a space with swings and see-saw for rainy days.

The second floor of the Children's House was given over to bedrooms. Besides the large room where I was staying with the other girls, and Sister Mary's room, there were two other large rooms with twin beds, dressers, chairs, and built-ins. At the end of the hall was a large attic with another huge set of drawers for storage. This was also used as a play area in bad weather.

The third floor was where the teenagers slept. It had two large rooms with three beds in each room, and a good sized hall with built-ins for the teens to use.

When plans were being made for my sister and me to go to the Shakers, my Godmother, Lucy O'Leary, become upset. She felt I should be placed in a Catholic home, either private or institutional. My mother would not give her consent for this since she felt that Ruth and I might be separated. I had made my First Communion a couple of years before and felt close to my Godmother. I would have been happy living with her, but she and her husband had a family of five, and were not wealthy. My mother had a good argument about our going to the Shakers. A few years before, she had placed two older children with the Shakers, Catherine, known as Katie, and Billy. She felt that as long as she held on to Ruth and me, there was hope that we all might be together again someday. But now Ruth and I were going to join the two older ones.

I scarcely knew Katie and Billy, since there had been few visits to the Shaker Village. A much older brother, Herbert, had come to the Shakers even earlier. Then Herbert had come home to help when my mother's health began to fail. Herbert was almost a surrogate father to Ruth and me, but by the time we went to the Shakers, he had joined the army.

It finally became evident to my Godmother that I would indeed be living with the Shakers. This, she felt sadly, was a real sin. At that time, Catholics had very fixed ideas about other religions. To even think of her Godchild going to a Religious Order to be cared for by people other than nuns was unimaginable. At this time, she told me that everyone had a guardian angel, and that I must rely on mine. I would find this to be true many times in the years to come. I named my angel G.A.

Two other sisters had come to the Shaker Community the year before. They were two and three years older than I was. The younger of the sisters, Lorraine, soon became my best friend, a friendship which would last a lifetime. After breakfast and our return to the Children's House, Sister Mary told Lorraine that she could show Ruth and me around the Shaker Village, but she cautioned her about taking us to the other side of the Village where the barns were.

As soon as we were outside, I asked Lorraine, "Why can't we go to the barns?" Lorraine told me that there was a bull in the barns and sometimes he got loose and chased people. That was enough to keep any city-bred child away. Later I discovered it was also because there were hired men and boys the Shakers cared for working in the barns.

The first place we visited was the Sisters' Shop, commonly called the Laundry. As we went past the rooms, I could see different ladies working on sewing. One person, who seemed unusually tall, was Sister Iona Sedgley who was of Indian descent and stood over six feet tall. As we were introduced, I looked up at her. It was a hot August day, and I recently had read that heat rises. Without thinking, I said, "You must be awfully hot today when the heat rises." Sister Iona laughed, and from that time was a good friend to me.

The laundry room was fascinating. Around one side of the

room were four sets of wooden tubs set in a circle. A huge washing machine made by the Shakers was on the other side of the room. Next to it was a large round wooden tub which was used for rinsing the clothes. On one end of the tub was a hand wringer. This tub was large enough for six people to stand in and still have room to move. This tub would be the cause of many of my future problems.

Sisters' Shop. Built in 1821. This building continues to house the Sisters' work rooms and the laundry.

My first dinner at the Shaker Community was at noon that Friday. This was a traumatic meal for me. I had been brought up in the Catholic Church at a time when it did not accept eating meat on a Friday. So it was a bit of a shock to be in the dining room and find meat on the table. I was in a dilemma. Should I go against the teachings of the Church and eat the meat, or should I try to get away with not eating it? I decided not to eat the meat. I was immediately offered the meat. I refused by saying, "I'm not very hungry." Then I was told that Shaker children ate what was on the table. With all eyes of the ten girls at the table watching me, I announced that I was sick and would like to leave the table. G.A. did not put up much of an argument, so I felt comfortable with the situation.

As evening came, and bedtime approached, it was time for the girls to say goodnight to Sister Mary, and to kneel by their beds for prayers. Each child said her own prayers silently. As had become my custom, I crossed myself when I finished praying. One of the other girls noticed and asked why I did this. Before I could answer, Sister Mary said, "It's because she was a Catholic when she lived with her mother, but now that she is a little Shaker girl she won't do that." Once again, I felt that I was in for a difficult time.

Then I noticed that all the girls were forming a line to go to kiss Sister Mary goodnight. I felt very uncomfortable about doing such a thing. The line became smaller, and I knew it would soon be my turn. Quickly, I rushed away to my room. As I climbed into bed, I called out, "Goodnight, Sister Mary."

When we got up on Saturday morning, I sensed a feeling among the older girls that had not been there before. Lorraine told me that Saturday was always "Mending Day." The older girls helped with the mending. They each did mending for a smaller child. My first summer was the last year that the girls would wear long cotton stockings. How the girls dreaded mending these long stockings! All of the girls learned to darn, and some of the older girls did a beautiful job. Katie was one of these, and she mended for both Ruth and me. Katie did not know us well at all, but her actions showed how much she cared for us.

The younger girls had the task of straightening up their drawers on Saturday mornings. The rest of the day was spent in play. There was much to do in the way of fun. Besides the seesaws and swings in the covered areas, there was a smooth field for ball games. "Tag" and "You're It" were other favorites.

One special place became a favorite of mine. It was a wide area of lilac bushes with extensive paths through it. Around the huge trunk were bench-like seats which Elder William had made years before. The ground was worn smooth by the many children who used this favorite spot. It was a good place to bring toys and set up tables with dishes. These gave the place the appearance of a tiny house. I had many happy hours in the "Lilac House," but it also would become the scene of one of my first catastrophes.

Chapter Two

❧ ❧ ❧

The Sabbath

As soon as dinner was finished on Saturday noon , Sister Mary called Ruth and me aside and told us that Sunday or the Sabbath actually began Saturday evening. No real work would be going on after five in the evening. The Sabbath would end at the same time on Sunday evening. No laundry would be left on the lines; all sewing rooms would be closed with the window shades drawn; and farm machinery would all be put away. Shaker Village would be neat and tidy for the Sabbath.

Sister Mary also told us that once each month on a Sunday she would call each of us for a private talk with her. This was called "Confession," which was an important part of the Shaker faith. This was a horrifying experience for most of the girls to look forward to because they had to talk about all the wrong things they had done since their last Confession. But this didn't bother me, since I had made my First Communion at the Catholic Church and had gone to Confession there. It would be much like the same experience of sitting in a dark room without seeing the priest.

On Saturday evenings the Shaker girls ten years and younger, which included me, studied their Sunday School lessons. At this time we used the *David C. Cook Bible Lessons*. The older girls read and studied from the *Testimonies of Mother Ann.*

On Sunday morning, breakfast was at 7:00 a.m., an hour later than usual. At ten minutes before ten, a bell rang. At this time, we were all to be quiet. We were to be in a "going to church" mood with no foolishness or unnecessary talk. We all wore attractive dresses. My grandmother always made clothes for Ruth and me. My dress was yellow, and Ruth wore pink. The younger girls wore pastel shades of dotted Swiss and dimity; the older girls were dressed in Shaker dresses of summer shades. We presented a charming picture: twelve girls, on their best behavior in their beautiful dresses.

As we walked into the large chapel in the Dwelling House, nearly all of the Community were there. The girls were usually the last ones to arrive. A bench at the back plus a row of small chairs were reserved for us. As we settled down, the clock struck ten and in came Eldress Prudence, Eldress Harriett Coolbroth, and Sister Jennie Mathers from the Sisters' entrance. At the same time, Brother Delmer Wilson came in from the Brothers' entrance. They marched slowly and solemnly to the front of the room where two benches faced the rest of the Community. When they arrived at their places, the whole assembly stood and Sister Della began to play the opening chords of the first hymn on the organ. Everyone, except the very youngest children, had a hymn book. I noticed that several boys sat with a Brother on the bench right in front of the Eldresses and Elder. Later I asked, "Why do the boys sit in the front while the girls sit in the back?" I was told that it was because the boys didn't like going to church and often misbehaved after the first hymn. By having them sit in front, it was easier to keep an eye on them.

After the first song, Brother Delmer read from the Bible, and then another song was sung. Next, Brother Delmer read from the Bible again. Sister Della sat at the organ during the Bible readings, and then she sat with the other Sisters. When Brother Delmer finished his second Bible reading, he began a sermon. The sermon seemed, to me and the other girls, to go on forever, especially on a warm summer morning.

Finally, Brother Delmer finished. There was then a brief time of quiet in order to give people time to think about the Bible readings and the words spoken by Brother Delmer. Then Eldress Prudence stood and spoke. She was always a picture in her long dress and cap, but on Sundays she was especially beautiful. She usually wore a deep purple Shaker dress, and she stood erect. Even the smallest child was impressed with her. It gave me the feeling of being in the presence of a queen.

After Eldress Prudence spoke, the Meeting was open to the working of the Spirit. Many of the Sisters spoke and there was a lot of singing. Later I learned that the girls usually spoke every other week. We would say a few lines of Scripture or a poem which Sister Mary gave us. The Community wanted us to do this so we would be in union with the Meeting. No one ever remembered the boys speaking in Meeting. Sometimes if I watched Sister Jennie, who took care of the boys, I could see her telling the boys to sing, but they never did.

After about an hour and a half, Meeting was over. The Eldresses and Elder stood and marched out. They were followed by the rest of the Community, beginning with the older Sisters who sat in the front row. I noticed that the older Sisters all wore caps. This was a good time for me to see everyone in the Community. They marched out in silence and did not speak until they came to the front hall.

Since Ruth and I were new to the Shaker Community, our pictures were taken after the Meeting was over. We went outside and Sister Mary took a picture of Ruth and me. Sometimes on Sundays, others would take pictures of the Sisters and Brothers since we were all dressed in our best clothes.

After the picture taking, we hurried back to our rooms to change our dresses before the bell rang for dinner. The bell always rang at 12:00 noon, and we didn't have much time to change. Because of the policy of having as little work as possible done on the Sabbath, the Sunday meals were simple and small. One of my vivid memories of Sunday dinners is that of Eldress Prudence and Sister Iona Sedgley cutting cheese to go with apple pie. This was a ritual at Shaker Village at this time. One of the Sisters working in the kitchen would go with Eldress Prudence to the storeroom where huge wheels of cheese were kept. A wheel of cheese was brought to the dining room. Sister Iona would choose the same sharp knife each time for cutting the cheese, and would slice the cheese. Eldress Prudence would arrange the sliced cheese on plates for the tables. Later when I worked in the kitchen, I asked why

The Girls' Order. This photograph was taken after Meeting sometime in 1938.

the cooks didn't serve the plates of cheese along with the other food. Others had asked the same question, but there never was an answer to it. It was simply one of those traditions of the Shaker family. And we loved any reason to have Eldress Prudence among us.

The first class of Sunday School was at 1:00 p.m. This was for the younger girls and Sister Mary taught us. At 2:00 p.m., Sister Della taught the teenagers. The rest of Sunday afternoon, we could do what we wanted to as long as it did not involve physical labor or play. Often I would read, and sometimes I would write letters. We were required to write to parents or other close family members every other Sunday.

Sunday was also the most common day for parents or other relatives to come and visit. The Children's House had a phone which was part of the phone system at the Community. Our ring was five rings. It was not uncommon to hear the five rings telling us that Mr. Smith was here to see his girls or Grandpa Merrill was waiting to see his granddaughter. Ruth and I had no visitors until several years later, when our grandmother would visit us.

Sunday's supper was an hour early at 5:00 p.m. It was a plain meal of baked potato with toasted codfish, and some preserved fruit such as pears or plums. To this day I have good memories of the codfish. It was a dried fish cut into strips, and somehow toasted to give it a special flavor. By the time I was old enough to wonder about the preparation, we were no longer having this as a Sunday night staple, and no one could tell me how it was actually prepared.

At 6:30 on Sunday evening, most of the Community gathered to learn and sing gospel hymns. We sang for about an hour. This was the end of the Sabbath.

Chapter Three

⭗ ⭗ ⭗

Some Early Memories

Monday was always wash day, when the laundry of the entire Community was done. This was possible even on rainy or stormy days because of the drying attics in the Sisters' Shop. Brother Delmer always rose earlier than normal on Mondays to start the fires in the wash room, and in the drying attic if the weather was bad. On Mondays we had a hearty breakfast of boiled eggs, which were cooked in a wire basket in the arch kettle in the kitchen. After breakfast those who would be doing the laundry gathered at the wash room. The original Shaker washing machine was used. It would be filled with sheets, towels, and such. The more personal laundry was done at the wooden tubs with wash boards. As each load of laundry was finished, it was lifted into the huge rinse tub, and put through a hand wringer. Then it was taken out of doors to the clothes drying yard situated just behind the Children's House.

The girls, ten years and older, helped with turning the wringer and carrying the laundry outside to dry. It was fascinating to work in the laundry. I heard all sorts of tales as well as the current gossip of the Sisters and older teenagers. The clothes drying yard was divided into areas in order to have room enough for everyone's clothes. We girls soon learned where not to hang our laundry. By early evening, the clothes were dry, and the lines were empty.

Tuesday morning, Brother Delmer would start fires in the ironing room before anyone, except the cooks, was up and about. Seeing the immense amount of ironing for the first time as a ten-year-old was mind boggling to me. The large room was furnished with sturdy Shaker-made tables. Each table was covered with a heavy Shaker woven blanket which in turn was covered with a sheet. The sheets used when I came here were those which had been made by the Shakers. A fireplace was directly under the massive brick warming oven which was lined with metal grates and had metal doors. This oven was filled with irons. Each individual iron was fitted with a handle in order to carry the hot irons to the tables. When we girls began using the irons, we were put at a table with an older girl or a younger Sister, who supervised our work. Lorraine and I began by ironing handkerchiefs, towels, napkins, and such.

The fireplace, directly under the heating oven, had to be stocked constantly with firewood to keep the irons hot. We girls would be sent to the woodshed in the basement to bring in more wood. This was always great fun. Once the fires were started in the morning, there was no further sign of Brother Delmer or the boys. It was strictly Sisters' work from there on.

A large wood burning stove occupied the middle of the ironing room to keep it comfortable during the cold months. My recollections, however, are of the ironing room being an extremely hot place.

As Lorraine and I worked in the ironing room, we listened to the other Sisters discussing Sister Muriel Barbarick, the Shaker school teacher who had such a large number of dresses. Sister Muriel spent most of the summer at Gorham Normal School taking classes to keep her teaching certification up to date. Because of this, she was not able to help with the laundry or to make her own dresses. A few of the Sisters had spent days making dresses for her, a task which had not been popular. I was especially eager to meet this school teacher who had so many dresses! After one of my first days in the ironing room, I had this opportunity. As Lorraine and I were on our way to the Sisters' Shop, Sister Muriel walked by us and spoke to us. We would see much more of her once school started.

Another interesting meeting took place during my first week at Shaker Village. One day, just as the noon meal was over, I saw my brother Billy leave the dining room with the other boys. I ran out after him because I had not had an opportunity to talk with him. I was surprised and shocked when one of the older girls came after me shouting, "You aren't supposed to talk with the boys!"

I quickly responded, "I'm not talking to 'the boys,' I'm just trying to speak to my older brother!"

Sister Mary soon arrived on the scene and reassured me that I hadn't done anything terribly wrong, but if I wanted to talk with my brother, she would arrange for me to have a visit with him at an appropriate time.

We girls worked in the ironing room only until the noon meal. In those days, there was an artesian well next to the Children's House. All of the drinking water for meals was pumped directly from the well. The water was always refreshingly cold and clear. On the hot days of summer, several pails of water were needed for use by the Family. A teenage girl and a younger girl would have the responsibility of bringing the water to the kitchen for a week at a time. This was one of my favorite things to do. My task was to pump the water, and my sister Katie, who was a large girl, would carry it into the Dwelling House.

When I first came to the Shakers, it was customary for an older or middle-aged Sister to be in charge of the dining room.

This Sister was usually one who was in ill health and could not do more active work. She would be assisted by two girls, one older and the other a very young child. After I had been at the Shaker Community about a week, I began working in the dining room with Sister Genie Coolbroth and a girl named Lucy. My task was to crumb the tables and assist in setting them. Each table was set for eight people. After the work of cleaning up from breakfast was finished, a large white sheet was placed over each table. At 11:45 a.m., I would go to the dining room and with the help of Sister Genie would remove the white sheet. This was a precarious task, since it was easy to be too rough and to send the glasses and other items crashing to the floor. Unfortunately, this was a favorite prank of many of the girls. When the older and younger girls who removed the covering cloth were in an impish mood, they would jerk the cloth off, sending tableware to the floor. Fortunately, the children usually used plastic glasses so no great harm was done. I was amazed at how understanding the Sisters were when this happened.

With the opening of school just a few days away, much attention was given to preparing clothes for the children to wear. Sister Mary and her assistant had been sewing pretty dresses, which were put in a closet which was a fairly large room. As children outgrew clothing, it was put in this closet, and was available for other children to wear. Many children came to the Shaker Community with only the clothes they wore. This communal closet always had dresses for the girls who needed them. Each girl had three dresses. We changed our school dresses immediately after school, and put on older clothes. The girls who were fourteen or older wore Shaker dresses.

One of the Sisters' industries at this time was candy making. They made candy and sold it at the Shaker Store, at the Poland Spring Inn, and on their many sales trips throughout New

England. One of the candies they made was maple sugar cakes. They purchased gallon pails of maple sugar for making these cakes. The candy was made in the Sauce Room at the Sisters' Shop. All the molds and equipment were kept in the Sauce Room, as well as a good number of pails of maple sugar.

One day several of us girls were looking in the various rooms of the Sisters' Shop, and we discovered the Sauce Room! The Sisters were hard at work, but they gave us a taste of the maple sugar candy. It was delicious! A few days later, we decided it would be a great idea to have a pail of maple sugar in our Lilac House where we could eat it whenever we wanted to. It was a great plan! That evening, before the Sisters' Shop was closed for the night, two of us took the matter into our own hands and took one of the pails of sugar to the Lilac House. The excitement we had in hiding this pail of maple sugar was like a shot of adrenaline. Somehow, through all of this we were able to escape the eyes of Sister Mary.

The next day we all went eagerly to have the forbidden treat, but when we got to the pail of maple sugar, it was covered with ants! It was heartbreaking to us. About the time that we made the discovery that the maple sugar wasn't fit to eat, Sister Elsie McCool made the discovery that a pail of maple sugar was missing! As the "new girl," every finger was pointed at me as the instigator of the situation. It had been my idea, but none of the other girls objected and they all had agreed with the idea.

Because this was considered a major wrongdoing, Sister Mary was not the person to deal with it. However, she was quick to show her displeasure with the whole affair. We were summoned to the room of Sister Jennie, the Second Eldress of the Community. With fear and trepidation, we went to her room at the Trustees' Office. We told her the whole story, and to our surprise and great relief, she burst out laughing! She laughed and laughed at the tragic way the ants had taken over what was to have been weeks of forbidden treats.

However, she did give us a severe lecture on the sins of taking what was not our property. She told us that the next time we wanted a sweet to come to her and she would give us candy. In addition to being Second Eldress, Sister Jennie was in charge of the candy industry. Some of the girls were awed by Sister Jennie, but I loved her at first sight, and would continue to find a great friend and mentor in her in the years to come.

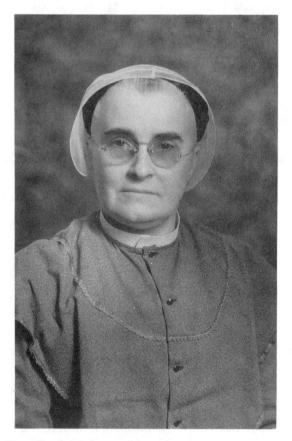

Sister Jennie Mathers, as I knew her.

Chapter Four

❧ ❧ ❧

The Shaker School

School started right after Labor Day. We began at 8:30 a.m.; had an hour off at noon; and ended the day at 4:00 p.m. My introduction to the Shaker School was disappointing. I had come from a small city school. I had read about country schools, and looked forward to walking a long distance to school. It was a surprise as well as a big disappointment to discover that the Shaker School was directly across the road from the Children's House.

The first day of school is always an exciting time, and my first day was no different. The school bell rang promptly at 8:30, and all twelve of us were in our new dresses and ready to begin. Sister Mary and her assistant had been sewing for days to outfit us for school. The Shaker girls were always as well dressed as the girls from the neighboring farms.

Sister Muriel was waiting for us. I soon learned that she was a stern person, and often she was terribly stern. However, she was an excellent teacher, and she felt that the students in the Shaker School had to excel with good grades. As far as teaching went, she was a fair person. If there were slow students, she spent extra time working with them.

The interior of the school was another surprise. It was a huge room dominated by an extraordinarily large wood burning stove in the middle. The stove also served as a room divider with the boys' desks on the south side and the girls' on the north side. A large piano filled the northeast corner. Years later, I discovered there was a window behind the piano. For many years, the Shaker School was the only school in the town of New Gloucester to boast of a piano. It had been purchased many years earlier; because of the desire to have one, the Shaker students gave programs and charged a fee for attending them. This money was saved until

School House. Built in 1880. The plans were drawn by Brother Hewitt Chandler and the building was constructed by the Brethren. Although located in the Community this was always a town school open to those who lived on this side of Sabbathday Lake. The town closed the building in 1950 when they consolidated the school system. The building was sold in 1957 to our neighbor, Mr. Harry Merrill. We were able to reacquire the building from Mr. Merrill's heirs in 1986. The building once again stands in its proper place in the village. Presently the school house houses the Shaker Library.

there was enough to purchase the piano.

The entire east wall of the school room was covered with blackboards and maps. The southeastern corner contained a large built-in sandbox for the little children. Between the entrance and the sandbox was a water jug. Depending upon the weather and the time of the year, the water jug was filled at the Dwelling House or the well next to the Children's House. There was no running water in the school house. Between the two windows on the south wall was another blackboard.

The west wall behind the boys' desks had shelves with books which formed the boys' library. The west wall behind the girls' desks had a cupboard which held books for the girls. These were books for enrichment and entertainment. They included Louisa May Alcott's *Little Men* and *Little Women.* These books helped to broaden our understanding of what life was like outside the shelter of a Shaker Community. We did use some of the books, especially the *Book of Knowledge* and a complete set of encyclopedias, in our school work.

Because there was no running water in the school house, we used outhouses as bathrooms. The ell on the west side of the school housed a wood shed which was always filled with good dry wood. On each side of the shed was an outhouse. One was for the girls and one for the boys. The outhouses were built high off the ground, and kept immaculately clean. I learned later that it was the responsibility of one of the hired men to keep this place clean and supplied with bathroom tissue. A large flat shelf separated the two seats, and each seat had its own cover. Once in a while, in good weather, we girls would sneak a Nancy Drew book out with us and read for a few minutes.

There were about twenty-eight students at the Shaker School this year. Two people sat at each desk. The chairs were close together, but I don't have any memories of students copying others' work. It would have been difficult to do this under Sister Muriel's eagle eye.

School always opened with everyone saying the Lord's Prayer in unison. Next, we repeated the pledge of allegiance to the flag. In addition to the flag inside the school room, there was a large flag pole in the school yard. A deserving student, in both scholarship and conduct, had the privilege of raising the flag. This honor was shared by a number of students.

My first day at the Shaker School was a day of planning and organizing classes. It wasn't one of my better days since I was automatically put back a grade. This was not because of my scholarship, but because I was the only one in my class. Sister Muriel felt it would be better to have three students in fourth grade rather than two in fourth and one in fifth. The following year there were only two of us in fifth grade: a neighborhood boy, Blynn Merrill, and myself. The two of us continued to be the only ones in our class for the rest of our time at the Shaker School.

The two older girls who had been helping in the kitchen during the summer now had new assignments. These two girls would be excused at 11:30 a.m. each school day to help with the noon meal. This was considered part of the Home Economics class.

When noontime came, we Shaker children had the opportunity to eat the noon meal with the Community. Sister Muriel had to have her meal delivered to her so she could be with the non-Shaker children who brought their lunches.

One might think it would be difficult to concentrate and study with so many classes in the same room, but I did not find this so. Work was especially easy for me my first year because I had been put back a grade. I also had the opportunity to listen to other classes, and I learned from that experience.

As I attended Shaker School, I discovered that it had many

special features. One of them was the walks which we took. We would go for walks as a group with Sister Muriel and an assistant, an older girl or a younger Sister from the Community. We would go to Aurelia's Falls in the woods; to the apple orchard in spring time when the apple trees were in bloom; and to other places. During these outings we learned about wildflowers, trees, and birds; we read about national events in the beauty of the apple orchard. Even though there were twenty-eight to thirty high-spirited students, there was never a behavior problem. If one misbehaved, that one was not allowed to go on walks in the future. And we all did love these excursions.

There were two recess periods at the Shaker School. The boys were first, and they had a period by themselves. The girls had recess at a later time. During recess we played organized games, baseball being one of the favorites.

Some of the Sisters who came to Sabbathday Lake from the Alfred Shaker Community worked at the Ministry's Shop during the day. The Ministry's Shop is situated next door to the Shaker School. These Sisters could look out the windows as they worked and watch the school children as they played. Eldress Harriett and Sister Eliza Jeffers had a sewing room which looked directly out on the playground. Watching the young people gave them much pleasure. As students, we had a reason to behave knowing we were watched as we played. Several of the children of the neighboring Cooper family spent time at the windows in conversation with the Sisters and grew close to them. To this day, the Coopers remain friends of the Shaker Community.

My first year at the Shaker School was not an especially happy time. I, like most of the children, did not care much for Sister Muriel. I probably had more grief from her than most of the other students. It was double jeopardy to know that whatever came up in school would be reported to the Sister taking care of me in the

Community. It was not easy knowing that Sister Mary would always be sure that I knew that she knew about my problems.

During my second year at the Shaker School, Sister Muriel began to have more problems with the older boys from the neighboring farms. The boys were typical fun loving kids, but Sister Muriel seemed unable to deal with that age group. During Christmas vacation of that year, Sister Muriel went to visit her sister and never returned. I can remember all the excitement in the Community and at the school; the scrambling around to find a teacher in the middle of the year; the conversations in the wash room and ironing room which would come to an abrupt stop when one of us young people came in. Even as children, we felt that something catastrophic had taken place when suddenly a teacher left in the middle of a term and never returned.

When school opened in January of 1940, history was being made. For the first time since the Shaker School opened, a person from the world was the teacher. In thinking back about that time, it is hard to give a reason for the change which came over the students. Perhaps we sensed that our new teacher was inexperienced. She appeared to be very young and was anxious to be friends with us rather than a teacher to us. Perhaps we felt a release from the extremely strict discipline we had experienced with Sister Muriel. Most likely, we felt freer knowing that this teacher was not a part of the Community and would not report our misdeeds to the caretakers. But whatever the reasons, we became extremely disorderly with our new teacher. To my chagrin and shame, we "took over."

Although our education appeared to be going forward as expected, there was a familiarity between student and teacher which should not have existed. We called our teacher by her first name when we felt like it. We took our time about coming into the school house when recess was over. The teacher should have gone straight to the Eldress and the parents of the non-Shaker students, but she didn't. Evidently, she wanted to bring us back into some sort of order on her own.

Sister Mildred, another Sister from Alfred, who was caretaker of the teenage girls, could see the school yard from her sewing room in the Sisters' Shop. She observed more than we suspected. She often asked why we were spending more time than usual at recess. From what we told her, she must have realized that we were not doing what was expected of us.

One day in early spring, my personal involvement came to a head. By this time we students had the upper hand. The teacher had planted a flower garden around the windows, and it had grown weedy. When I did something out of order, the teacher told me that as a punishment I was to go out and work in the little garden. I replied, "It's not up to me to work in your garden!"

"You will work in the garden or leave for the day," she responded.

I chose to leave and walked out of the school. I went to find Sister Mildred and told her that I had been expelled from school. She told me that I had the choice of going back to school and apologizing to the teacher or staying home and helping the other girls with the spring house cleaning. Without hesitation, I chose to help with the cleaning.

At noontime, when the older girls were sitting out in the sun, I sat among them feeling my importance. The teacher ate her lunch at the Trustees' Office. When she came to school for the afternoon session, she saw me on the porch. She called to me as though nothing had happened, "Frannie, you can come back to school this afternoon."

I was buoyed up by the presence of the older girls and replied, "Only my friends call me Frannie!"

In the days to come, this became a byword, and was often

referred to when a similar situation arose. I spent the afternoon cleaning house, and that evening had a long session with Sister Mildred. On Monday, I went back to school and nothing more was ever said about the matter.

In September of 1941 another new teacher took over. This teacher was to have a wonderfully good influence on my life. Mrs. Stoddard, now deceased, was older than our former teacher and lived in Lewiston. She was married to a Serviceman and because of the war was under much personal strain. From the very beginning she had good rapport with the students. Physically she was lovely, one of the most attractive women I had known. She inspired all of us to do our best. She opened up so many new ways of teaching that school became a joy for even the slowest learner.

During her time at the Shaker School, I was given charge of the little ones, the children of the tenant farmers. Once my own school work was completed, I would work with these little ones under the supervision of Mrs. Stoddard. I loved this work. Other opportunities opened to me. Mrs. Stoddard's husband would be able to visit her occasionally. When she had to take him back to the base, she would be late for school. It was arranged that when this happened, I would open school and take charge of things until she arrived.

The older girls and boys who might have presented a problem had finished Shaker School. I cannot remember a single time when trouble developed when I was substituting for Mrs. Stoddard. On occasion I was referred to as "teacher's pet." I was so happy to assist this wonderful teacher who had brought so much into my life, that being called "teacher's pet" only added to my feeling of well-being. It was amazing how the Shaker School became a well run place of learning with the right management and fair discipline.

Once again, the extracurricular aspects of school became possible. The whole school body spent a lovely day at the cottage on Sabbathday Lake. Then, when the end of the school year approached, Mrs. Stoddard arranged with the kitchen staff to have a picnic for all the students at our Shaker cottage, Camp Jennie.

Mrs. Stoddard was part of a musical family of Italian ancestry. Her father and sister were also talented musicians. As gas rationing allowed, they would come to our school for musical programs. At this same time, we were blessed with Miss Gillette, an extraordinary music teacher from the school district. With Mrs. Stoddard and Miss Gillette, we began exploring the work of Gilbert and Sullivan, Sigmund Romberg, and John Philip Sousa. I remember "God Bless America" being sung daily.

If it had not been for the war, Mrs. Stoddard would have continued at the Shaker School. She liked her situation, and the Shakers and parents of the neighborhood students were more than satisfied with her. However, times were uncertain, and after two years Mrs. Stoddard left Maine to be with her husband in California before he was sent overseas.

The Sisters and Brothers in charge of the young people were the ones to decide when those under their care should leave Shaker School and continue their education within the Community. Fortunately for me, I graduated from Shaker School when Mrs. Stoddard left. I think it would have been difficult for me to continue with any other teacher. Mrs. Stoddard had come into my life at a vulnerable time and had a positive effect on my attitudes and all of my life.

My graduation was lovely although bittersweet. I knew that never again would I have the daily contact with not only my favorite teacher of all time, but with favorite students from the world, especially the little students with whom I had worked. Sister Mildred made me a lovely new white Shaker dress with red polka dots. A young Sister, who had a gift of flower arranging, made me a beautiful bouquet of lilies of the valley and other seasonal flowers.

The teacher and students of the Shaker School taken on the last day of school June 1940. The teacher, Miss Fickett, is the third from the left in the back row. I am the first person on the right in the back row.

Graduation Day. Left to right Frances, Frederick Akins (Superintendent of Schools), Evelyn Stoddard (teacher), Miss Gillette (music teacher), Blynn Merrill.

Chapter Five

🌢 🌢 🌢

Eldress Prudence

With the exception of Sister Mildred Barker, probably no other person had a greater influence on my years growing up at Shaker Village than Eldress Prudence Stickney. Although I loved her dearly and had a close friendship with her, it has only been in later years that I have come to realize what a privilege this was. We did not realize it at the time, but with Eldress Prudence working around the Community, we were witnessing first hand one of the truly great Sabbathday Lake Eldresses.

Eldress Prudence was the only person at Shaker Village whom I felt I knew a little when I arrived. This was because my brother Herbert, who was eighteen years older than I, had lived at the Shaker Community years before Ruth and I came. He and Eldress Prudence were good friends. One wonders what brings together a young person and a much esteemed older person. But whatever the reason, the two of them shared an unusual and wonderful relationship. Much later, I was to have the same privilege.

At eighteen, Herbert had left the Shaker Community and come home to help my mother. Unfortunately, this did not last, because, like many young men at that time, he joined the military when war first reared its ugly head. But while Herbert was home,

I heard a lot about Eldress Prudence, and she continued their friendship through correspondence.

During my first day, I spotted Eldress Prudence at the dinner table. On the second day, I made my way to say hello to her, much to the chagrin of Sister Mary and the other girls. I did not realize at the time that a child of ten did not voluntarily seek out and speak to the Eldress. Eldress Prudence, however, did not seem to mind in the least; I think she was rather pleased. It must have been difficult and lonely for her, the ranking head, to be in a situation where position and duties removed her from the general population of the Community.

I will never know for sure if my seeking her out that day made her aware of me, or if it was her natural instinct of knowing when a person, especially a child, was in need of special attention. No matter what, from the beginning, Eldress Prudence was a friend indeed. She was the only one ever to call me Frahn-cess, except for my mother who came from Scotland.

Often children see things which escape adults, and I saw and felt that Eldress Prudence enjoyed having me seek her out. As a result, I did not discontinue what appeared to others to be shockingly bold conduct on my part. When things became tough at the Children's House, which was quite often, the other girls would say to me, "Why don't you go and tell Eldress Prudence?" The girls felt that Eldress Prudence would listen to me, but I never felt I could do that. Even at my early age I realized that union was necessary to the life of the Community. I realized that Eldress Prudence in her wise actions and great understanding would not tolerate a child complaining about the Sister in charge. However, she must have been aware of the situation, and in her wisdom used other ways to make life happy for me.

After I had been in the Community for a while, a call came that Eldress Prudence wished to see me in her sitting room. This would be the first time I had ever ventured into her private quarters. I had mixed feelings as I walked up the two flights of stairs. Had I been too forward? Had Sister Mary taken all the defiance she could from me? Would I be asked to leave? Questions flew through my mind as I walked into her room.

Eldress Prudence was sitting in a small straight backed Shaker rocker. She asked me to sit in a Shaker rocker opposite her. A small woman, Eldress Prudence always wore dresses which came just above her black, tied shoes. She had a lace cap on her head and wore a Shaker knit cardigan. Even in warm weather, Eldress

Eldress Prudence Stickney. This photograph was taken in Eldress Prudence's sitting room in the Dwelling House.

Prudence always wore a sweater. She was knitting. I never knew her to simply sit with folded hands.

She looked at me and said, "Frances, I have a favor to ask you. Would you be willing to meet me at the north door every morning except Saturdays and Sundays, and carry my work basket as you accompany me to the Sisters' Shop?"

Of course I said I would! How could anyone turn down such a special assignment, particularly a child who was finding life difficult at Shaker Village? I felt as if a great honor had been bestowed upon me.

When I got back to the Children's House, the other girls were waiting to see what terrible judgment had come upon me. At that time, no one could remember ever knowing of a child who had been called to an Eldress' sitting room. Usually any contact between the children and an Eldress was done through the Sister in charge of the children.

Eldress Prudence was a frequent traveler to the resort hotels around the State, so there were many days when she did not go to the Sisters' Shop. However, on the days she went, I would always be waiting for her at the door. It never occurred to me to wonder how she carried her basket back to the house at noontime.

During the summer months when Eldress Prudence went to the resort hotels, she was often away for several days at a time. She was usually accompanied by Sister Iona Sedgley or Sister Eva Libby. These summer sales trips took the Shaker Sisters to resort hotels at York Beach, Boothbay Harbor and Monhegan Island in Maine and to the White Mountains in New Hampshire. These trips sounded exciting to me, and I looked forward to going on them when I was old enough, but by then there were not as many sales trips being made.

Besides these sales trips, the Sisters took fancy goods, flowers, and other things to the Poland Spring House and Summit Springs two or three times a week. In the fall, Sister Della was often a judge at the Cumberland Fair, the Oxford Fair, and the Eastern States Exposition in Springfield, Massachusetts. One of the major sales was the Christmas sale at the old Columbia Hotel in Portland. This was a three-day affair, and was the last source of financial income for the year.

Sister Mildred always asked us if we wanted to make some special item for Eldress Prudence to sell at this fair, and of course we did. We had a lively time choosing what we would make. The night before the sale, we all would assemble in Eldress Prudence's room to present our gifts. It was like an early Christmas with one person receiving all of the gifts. She would exclaim over each handmade item, and we girls couldn't have been happier, feeling a bit like the Magi of old.

As I have mentioned, Eldress Prudence was a tiny person who ate very little, at least in front of the Community. We did learn, however, that on her weekly trips to Portland, accompanied by a younger Sister, Lillian Beckwith, she would always go to Woolworth's for lunch and eat a huge banana split. It was taken for granted that Lillian would never divulge this very human trait, but when it did become known, we loved it! It made Eldress Prudence become a little more human and down to earth to us. To my knowledge, no one ever let Eldress Prudence know that we knew her secret. I have always loved the mental image of Eldress Prudence climbing up on the high stool and digging into one of my favorite treats.

This next incident is one which has been told to few people through the years. One Sunday morning while I was still in the Children's House, I was sitting in the last row in the Chapel at Meeting. We had almost come to the end of the service when suddenly Sister Eliza Jeffers, a gentle and unassuming Sister from Alfred, leapt from her place in the second row and almost without touching the floor, was immediately in front of Eldress Prudence, Eldress Harriett, and Sister Jennie. She began to whirl around in a small circle. Eldress Prudence went to her, and without touching her, gave her invisible support. This whirling lasted a brief time, and during that time not a sound was heard in the Chapel. The amazing thing was that even the young people never made a sound. Without a doubt, it was the manifestation of the Spirit, and every person in the room felt it. Soon the Meeting ended, and Eldress Prudence led Sister Eliza out of the room. Sister Eliza appeared to be exhausted and pale. The entire Community left the room more quietly than usual.

When we got back to the Children's House, Sister Mary told us that Sister Eliza had been under the power of the Spirit, and, even if she had wanted to, she could not have controlled or stopped the whirling which occurred. To my knowledge, this was the last

Sister Eliza Jeffers. You can see the rear of the Ministry Shop in the background where Sister Eliza and the other Alfred Sisters had their work rooms.

time such a happening, which had been common in earlier times, occurred within Shakerism.

Eldress Prudence was a wonderful combination of great wisdom and humility which set an example of what the word "ministry" is all about. Ministry, of course, simply means to serve, and Eldress Prudence portrayed this in many ways. Because of her dignity, which was a hallmark of her character, she made the words of the well-known Shaker song, "Simple Gifts", come to life: "'Tis the gift to be simple, 'tis the gift to be free, 'Tis the gift to come down where we ought to be." When this little lady appeared in the Community kitchen each morning at 11:30, to wash the pots and pans which had accumulated, this rare combination of dignity and simplicity came to the forefront. She, in her infinite wisdom, realized that this time of day, just before the serving of the major meal of the day, was often a difficult time. This was especially true during the hot summer months. Her presence in the midst of the busyness, doing the distasteful chore of cleaning the pots and pans, was a revelation to me as a young person. She was affectionately dubbed the "Kitchen Angel," with good reason.

In looking back over the years, one has to wonder just how much kitchen work the young Prudence had been involved in. Everywhere in the kitchen and dining room were, and still are, signs which show that much of the layout was planned with her in mind. When I wondered why the original old iron sink in the kitchen and the slate sink in the dining room were set at such a low angle, I was told they were placed with Eldress Prudence in mind.

This also explained her special interest in kitchen-related items. Never did she go away for any length of time without bringing back a gift to be used in the kitchen or dining room: a special silver tea strainer, a set of cheese plates, and a lovely set of fruit plates come to mind. In those days there was uniformity about most items. Cheese plates were used for cheese and fruit plates for fruit. This may seem a bit overdone, but with sixty or seventy people eating, such rules allowed Community life to proceed in an orderly fashion.

Eldress Prudence never fully relinquished her involvement with kitchen and food matters. Besides slicing the cheese each Sunday, she and Sister Iona would fill the various containers of staples, sugar, flour, coffee, and such, each Monday morning. They would gather the pails and containers and fill them for the week. These canisters and sugar barrels still exist in the kitchen "storeroom" at the north end of the lower hall.

If Eldress Prudence had a hobby, it was correspondence. She loved writing to people, and sat at her table in her sitting room well into the evenings keeping up with correspondence. She was friendly with people from every walk of life; the common person, members of the Legislature, Governors, and even Presidents. Among her famous correspondents were the governor of Maine, Lewis O. Barrows, and President Herbert Hoover. During Hoover's ill fated Presidency, she regularly kept in touch with him, reassuring him of her support. It is doubtful that he was the avid correspondent which she was, but that did not seem to deter her or daunt her. When a member of his staff wrote, it was a red letter day. We have never been able to fathom if it was his political style that appealed to her, or the fact that he was a Quaker. Whatever the reason, their friendship finally resulted in Hoover's coming for a visit to Shaker Village after leaving the Presidency.

Herbert Hoover's coming was an exciting day for the entire Community and the surrounding area. It made no difference that Hoover was no longer President; he had been. The Shaker School was closed for the afternoon, and all of the students, including those from the neighboring farms, were invited to attend the reception for Hoover and his entourage in the music room of the Dwelling House. His arrival was announced with sirens and motorcycle officers bearing down on Shaker Village. There were picture taking sessions, the usual excitement of school children meeting a famous person, and then off they sped to wherever they were going next. Unfortunately, the photos taken during this momentous visit were lost, strayed, or stolen. It is only in the memories of Sister Minnie and myself that this exciting event is remembered.

Eldress Prudence and the other older Sisters were friendly with Governor and Mrs. Barrows. One day Eldress Prudence, Sister Jennie and Sister Iona traveled to the Blaine House to have lunch with the Barrows. Later, Mrs. Barrows presented them with a large photo of the group, taken at the Blaine House. For years the photo hung in the music room.

Each summer, a concert was presented by Gove's Band, which was an orchestra at the Poland Spring resort. Because of Eldress Prudence, this band offered to present a concert at Shaker Village. What a spectacular sight it was! The members of the band were on the front steps and lawn of the Dwelling House, with the Community and friends seated on the lawns and steps of the Meeting House across the road. The band members wore sparkling white uniforms with gold trim. The pastel colors of the Sisters' dresses as well as those of the children and older girls, created a setting with which Renoir would have been pleased. A reception, to which we all were invited, followed after the concert.

In December of 1940, a large celebration was planned for Eldress Prudence's eightieth birthday. Many festive arrangements had been made, but other events were being set in motion which would have great impact on this Community, although at the time it was not apparent. The Community was called together and informed that Gertrude M. Soule would be arriving in

*Mrs. Barrows with the Sisters. Governor Barrows had invited Eldress
Prudence to the Blaine House for Luncheon. Left to right—Mrs.
Barrows, Eldress Prudence Stickney. Back row same order—Sister Iona
Sedgley, Sister Eva Libby, Sister Jennie Mathers.*

Portland via bus and would take up residence in the Community. Gertrude had come here when she was seven years old, but had left to live in the world on April 18, 1925. Although contact by the Community with those who chose to leave was not encouraged, Gertrude had managed to keep in touch with Eldress Prudence and others through the years. Her return was to be a birthday gift to Eldress Prudence. (In later years, Gertrude would become Eldress and still later would fill a role in the Ministry.) Sister Mary was still caring for the little girls, and Gertrude became her assistant. Her bedroom was in the Dwelling House, but her days were spent in the room directly over the children's work and play room at the Children's House. This was the room she had used before leaving the Community. By this time I was living in the Dwelling House with the teenagers under Sister Mildred's care.

Governor and Mrs. Lewis Barrows were expected guests for Eldress Prudence's eightieth birthday celebration. Unfortunately, just hours before the event, the Governor had to cancel for an emergency meeting. Mrs. Barrows, however, driven in a State car by a uniformed chauffeur, arrived in the midst of a very stormy evening. She brought with her a huge birthday cake decorated with a circle of miniature blue State of Maine flags. A special birthday program was presented by the Community. I still remember how nervous we all felt about having the Governor's wife in the audience.

In looking back, I marvel at the wisdom and understanding of this person who had the responsibility and care of the spiritual and material welfare of about sixty people.. In spite of the fact that I enjoyed a closeness with Eldress Prudence, I never lost sight of the fact that she was the spiritual leader of the Community. She was an individual who inspired the greatest respect and awe in all who knew her. When I was with her, I felt I was in the presence of a saintly person.

Chapter Six

ᕯ ᕯ ᕯ

Hands to Work

While I was still living at the Children's House, I was assigned to a job which I really loved, but which caused a bit of envy on the part of some of my peers. I was to go to the Trustees' Office and help with cleanup and dishes in the hired men's dining room. Just the fact that I would be going to the Trustees' Office was exciting! It was a place where the young people seldom went; a place where one was summoned to visit company from the world; a place for a serious session with Sister Jennie. To be asked or expected to go to the Trustees' Office five days a week was a bit mind boggling. During this time, 1939, work at the great mill was still very much active. Part of the pay for the men who worked there was the noon meal, a hearty meal.

I remember six people sitting around the table. There were loads of dishes to wash. I enjoyed every moment I spent there. The food offered to these hard working men was different from what the Community ate, and I could usually have leftovers.

In looking back, what I enjoyed most was the conversation. I must have made the mistake at times of entering into the talk, since I remember being told that I talked too much. In other words, I was there to work and not to talk.

I never left without making my way to see Sister Jennie Mathers, a dear soul whom I loved dearly. Sister Lillian Beckwith, Mary's natural sister, was in charge of guests staying at the Trustees' Office. In addition, she worked full time in the Shaker Store, and was assistant postal clerk. It was Sister Lillian whom I was helping as she and Sister Jennie prepared and cooked the meals for the hired men.

Sister Lillian was a lovely and unusually attractive woman, and had many friends from the world because of her work at the Shaker Store and with the guests. She was a role model for me and I loved being with her. Because I was with her several hours a day, I observed that she was not a very happy person. In spite of our age difference, we talked a great deal, and I should have been prepared when she left the Community shortly after Eldress Prudence died.

Trustees' Office. Built in 1816 as the "Second House" this building was used as the residence of the older Brethren and Sisters until 1880 when it became the Office. The building still serves as the Office. The Shaker Store is located here and guests of the Community stay here as well.

Her leaving was a tremendous loss to me personally, and to the Community as well. She filled many places requiring the gift of meeting and dealing with the public. Her sister continued on in the work here for another few years.

One day as I was on my way to the Trustees' Office, I passed a Sister sitting in the shade by the sun porch of the Dwelling House. She was knitting an attractive sweater, and I stopped to say hello. She told me she was Sister Mildred, and for the time being was sleeping in the Trustees' Office. "But why haven't I seen you before?" I asked.

"I've been very ill and have been recuperating," she answered. "In a few weeks, as soon as I become stronger, I'll be taking a group of girls from the Children's House to be under my care in the Dwelling House." Sister Mildred continued, "I'm already responsible for a few teenagers in the Dwelling House, but my assistant, Sister Mabel, is caring for them until I am well again," she added.

We seemed to like each other right away. "Your sister Katie will be one of the girls coming from the Children's House," she announced.

"Can I come, too?" I begged

"You are still too young, but if you try to be good, the time will pass quickly, and you, too, will be able to come," Sister Mildred responded.

I was disappointed, but I also was encouraged to know that at some time I would be going to the Dwelling House.

In the weeks that followed, I saw a lot of Sister Mildred, my new friend. She had a sewing room in the Sisters' Shop, the same room which she had until she died. I would steal away during recreation or free time and sit and talk with her. Sister Mary was not very happy when I did this. My best friend Lorraine, who was two years older than I, usually went with me to visit Sister Mildred.

When I heard that Lorraine would be one of the girls leaving the Children's House to be under Sister Mildred's care, I felt hurt, left out, and somewhat jealous. Sister Mary was never pleased that Lorraine and I were such good friends. It may have been that she felt we were not a good influence on one another when one of us was upset. Sister Mary probably thought that moving Lorraine into the Dwelling House would allow our friendship to fade away. But it did not turn out that way. Lorraine and I found ourselves working the same kitchen shifts, and we were also together in school. Our friendship was too deep to be destroyed.

Sister Olive Dobson was a Sister from Alfred who had her sewing room in the Ministry's Shop. She loved cats. We girls did not especially care for her. We had a favorite cat that usually stayed near our Children's House. Soon we noticed our cat was always going across the road to the Ministry's Shop. Why would our cat do this? The mystery was solved when we saw Sister Olive enticing

Lucinda, Lorraine, Ruth and me with our kittens.

the cat across the road with food she had brought from the dinner table. Naturally, our cat soon became her cat, and we girls were not happy about this "catnapping." We let Sister Olive know that we felt she had stolen our pet. And so there was not the friendliest attitude between Sister Olive and the younger girls.

I continued to cause problems at the Community. One of our favorite summer activities was going to the beach at Sabbathday Lake for the day. Because of the large number of girls, the younger girls went on Mondays and the older ones on Tuesdays.

One Monday while I was exploring the shore at the lake, I discovered a enormous old tree with a hollow in the trunk. An idea came to my mind immediately! It would be the perfect place to leave a message for another person. A plan of action soon formed in my mind. I would write letters to Lorraine and leave them in the hollow of the tree on Mondays. Lorraine could find them on Tuesdays when she came to the beach, and she could leave a letter for me.

This was great fun for the two of us, and for the next three weeks we eagerly looked forward to writing and receiving our letters. Then Sister Olive, our chaperone for the day, saw me taking a letter from the tree and reading it. She imagined the worst and reported me to Sister Mary. When I told my story to Sister Mary, she refused to believe me. She felt that I could not have received a note from a friend at the Community. She believed that I was having contact with someone outside the Community. As a result, I was punished by not being allowed to go to the beach on Mondays.

As a result of the letter incident at the lake, we girls ganged up against Sister Mary. How could we get even for what we felt was an injustice? We girls talked at length, and we considered many suggestions. One of the girls suggested that I go to Eldress Prudence with the whole story, but I felt that this was not the way

Girls and Sisters enjoying a picnic in the pines by the lake.

to go. I knew that Eldress Prudence would never pit a child against a caretaker and rightfully so. I told the others that I would think of something. The perfect solution came to my mind when I was helping Sister Genie Coolbroth in the dining room.

I was learning the proper way to set a table according to Shaker custom. At that time, a tea cup was placed at the table setting of each person. While Sister Genie's back was turned, I quickly spit into Sister Mary's cup, not a lot but just a quick spit. I was on "pins and needles" the rest of the day waiting for supper and my vindication. I was probably foolish in letting the others know ahead of time what I had done, but I couldn't resist telling them. That night when we sat at the table, eight pairs of eyes were on Sister Mary's tea cup. When the unfortunate victim took her first swallow, a huge sigh of relief went up from the children's table.

While I was in the children's order, I learned to do various kinds of work. As children we cut up the balsam for the fir balsam pillows, and we were all taught to knit. As I mentioned previously, we all learned to mend as well. We mended the feet of the long stockings which were part of our dress. On birthdays, each little girl was given a sewing or knitting bag for her own use. These bags were made of bright calico, some with prints and others plain. The bag had a drawstring for closing. We hung our bags on our own pegs on the wall in the children's activity room of the Children's House.

One of the special items we made as children was the jump rope with soft handles. We would fill the handles with a soft stuffing. Unfortunately, we don't have a single jump rope in our collection today.

As the girls approached their early teens, some of them were gifted with sewing skills. These girls learned to use the sewing machine which enabled them to help Sister Mary make dresses for the younger girls. I was not especially drawn to sewing, but I loved to knit and do samplers.

Mending the socks was universally disliked, but, like it or not, everyone of us was expected to learn this form of sewing. One time on mending day, Saturday, my little sister Ruth asked Sister Mary, "Why are you always grumpy on Saturdays?"

Sister Mary replied, "It's not me that's grumpy. You are all so worked up over this hated task, that you are the grumpy ones."

My little sister Ruth became proficient in mending, but to this day I still cannot do a neat job of mending. My older sister, Katie, usually took pity on me and would sneak my mending in with her own.

As I mentioned earlier, we girls helped with the laundry. It seemed that every time I helped with the laundry, I would always come up with one sock missing; this was a real trial to me. The Shakers never have believed in corporal punishment, and so the two most used punishments were no day at the beach in the summer, or no Thursday night movies in the winter. I really looked forward to the Thursday night movies in the Dwelling House, but I missed many a movie. After quite a few missed socks and an equal number of missed movies, I was missing a sock again on laundry day. I was beside myself! Another missed movie! After roaming around the wash room and drying attics looking for my missing sock, I sat on the edge of the Shaker washing machine and felt a real sense of despair. I was about to miss another movie, which was one of the "Our Gang" series, one of my favorites.

I decided to call on G.A.'s help. A message came to me that a prayer might help. In the wash room, all by myself, I decided to pray for help in finding the stocking which was causing me so much grief. When a young person didn't show up for the movies, there were only two possible reasons for the absence: sickness or punishment. Everyone knew I wasn't sick, and it was humiliating for the entire Community to know I was being punished yet again. As I sat there wondering where to look next, something, I'm sure it was G.A., told me to take a real good look in the bottom of that horrible old tub, because somewhere in the depths of that huge, awful tub was a missing sock. I looked again, and sure enough, tucked away in a corner, and not easily seen because the sock and tub were both dark, was my missing sock! It was damp and wrinkled, but I grasped it with delight and ran to Sister Mary! To her credit, she accepted the grimy sock, and I went to the movies.

I wish I could say I never lost a sock again during my growing up, but I can say this was a turning point for me as far as having faith in prayer. My life from then on never seemed quite as difficult. I knew that G.A. would be there when I needed special help. I was convinced that if prayer could lead me to a sock in a dark tub, it could help me with all of my other "dark tubs" along the way.

Besides these tasks, which went on daily, there were other, unexpected things in which I was involved. Sister Ethel took a fancy to me and often requested that I help with some work which she was doing. The phone would ring at the Children's House, and Sister Ethel would say, "I need a pair of willing hands and would like Frances to come over to the Meeting House and help me with chairs."

Sister Ethel was an expert at taping the seats of Shaker chairs. When I worked with her, I helped pull the tape through. I loved working with her, and she was another Sister who made me feel special. At this time, Sister Ethel was caretaker of the small Museum

Sister Ethel Peacock known to us as Sister "Grandmother."

which was housed in the upper floors of the Meeting House. The Meeting room itself was used to store the extra furniture which had come from the Alfred community when they joined Sabbathday Lake in 1931. This furniture was sold to people from the world. Sister Ethel was a sociable person and loved to talk with people. At that time, not more than half a dozen people would come to the Museum in an afternoon. Sister Ethel would usually dismiss me from the Meeting room when someone came, but sometimes she would forget to, and I would sit quietly in the blue built-in pews. I had a fascinating time watching and listening to the people who had come to buy Shaker-made items. It was there that I first saw some of the early Shaker collectors. It is especially interesting to look back at and reflect on the prices which some pieces brought at that time.

Before I left my home in Lewiston to come to Shaker Village, a tremendous fire had swept through much of the neighboring city of New Auburn. It leveled a large part of the city. After the fire and smoke had cleared away and cleanup had begun, what was left looked like a ghost town. This was a scary experience for me.

Twice during the two years I lived at the Children's House, I experienced the same type of fear. One time was when the Gray Plains, just south of the Village, were on fire and the smoke was visible at the Village. I began to think that maybe all of the property leading to Shaker Village and the Village itself would be consumed in flames. Of course, it turned out to be an entirely different situation than the one in Auburn. The fire on the Gray Plains caused the blueberries to grow to enormous size and in great abundance. Two years later, as an older girl, I would go to the Gray Plains to pick blueberries.

The other frightening situation was when the 1938 hurricane struck Maine in a deadly way. As the hurricane was beginning and the winds were growing stronger, I remember begging to be allowed to stay out of doors for a bit longer. I have always loved to walk in the wind, and even at that early age it was exciting to me. There was a tremendous amount of activity in the Village. The Brothers, boys and Sisters were all hurrying about preparing to "batten down" the property. We, like all children, reveled in an out-of-the-ordinary happening. We were running around in the area between the Sisters' Shop and the Children's House when all of a sudden the chimney of the Sisters' Shop began falling. At the same time, parts of the roofs of the Sisters' Shop, the Sisters' Wood Shed, the Brothers' Wood Shed, and the east side of the Ministry's Shop began flying through the air. Without any warning, we were surrounded with debris which had been caught up in the fierce winds. It was a scene I will long remember. In what seemed like only seconds, trees also began coming down. We children were shrieking and trying to reach the safety of the Children's House. Poor Sister Mary was beside herself as she tried to be heard above the wind. She called us to come quickly. We had ignored her earlier calls to us, choosing rather to be part of the excitement outside. We received a well deserved scolding about minding when we were spoken to. At both of these events, the fire and hurricane, G. A. was very much pressed for help.

The 1938 hurricane did much damage to the Shaker Village. The *Church Family Journal* records that for days after, work was being done to repair the buildings and grounds. Although Maine was hit badly by this storm, worse damage was done in other New England states. Reports reached us later that Canterbury Shaker Village had received tremendous losses of buildings as well as timber. In later years, I learned that this hurricane was the beginning of the end financially for the Canterbury Shaker Village.

During the two years I lived at the Children's House, six individuals left the Community. Most were young people. For several years, there was a constant turnover at Shaker Village with new arrivals and others leaving. The two years I spent at the Children's House may not have been the happiest of my life, but they certainly were interesting years.

Chapter Seven

ᴏ ᴏ ᴏ

I Move to the Dwelling House

One day about two years later, I came home from school to find that most of my personal belongings had been packed into baskets and boxes. I heard the exciting news, "You will be moving to the Dwelling House tomorrow." This was the news I had been waiting for!

I was the youngest of the group and had been allowed to move into the Dwelling House sooner than most. This was due to the wise and kind counsel of Eldress Prudence who realized that life at the Children's House had become a very unhappy existence for me.

As I went to sleep for the last time at the Children's House, I had mixed emotions. I was thrilled that I would be in the Dwelling House with the older girls, but I had a bit of remorse that I had not been able to relate more compatibly with Sister Mary. I had a feeling of sadness that I was leaving my little sister Ruth behind. She, however, had adjusted well in her life at Shaker Village and was already helping with the younger girls. I knew it would be only a matter of a few years before she would follow me to the Dwelling House.

The move from the Children's House to the Dwelling House was made early on a Saturday morning. This was to give the young person a chance to adapt to new living conditions before school began on Monday. Mercifully, the early Saturday move was an opportunity to escape the mending session which usually took up most of my Saturdays.

Any hope of rooming with Lorraine soon vanished. To my surprise, I discovered that I would be alone in a small room. Because of the large group of girls who were already under Sister Mildred's care, there was little space left. My small room opened into a large room occupied by Sister Della Haskell and Sister Helena Lovely. Sister Helena left the Community the following year. Evidently, my room had been intended as a young person's room with the Sister in charge of her living in the larger room. All of the other girls shared a room with three people. These were large rooms, and the girls weren't crowded. Each room had seven drawers in the built-ins.

Upon moving to the Dwelling House, one of the first people I had close contact with was a young Sister named Mabel Lovely, a sister to Helena. I had been aware of Sister Mabel earlier, since she was always in charge of the older girls' day at the lake, and was one of the cooks in the kitchen when I was doing dining room duty.

Sister Mabel was Sister Mildred's assistant, and she went everywhere the girls went: to the lake, to the garden, or wherever we went. Sister Mildred was responsible for ten young people. She was still not in the best of health, but had assumed the responsibility of the young people under Eldress Prudence's persuasive urging. Sister Mildred depended greatly on Sister Mabel, and a more perfect choice would have been difficult to find. Sister Mabel was full of life, outgoing, and related well to all types of personalities. She was a best friend to all of us girls through those formative years which are so important to teenagers. My life was greatly influenced by Sister Mabel. Sister Mildred was in charge

Dwelling House. This was the second Dwelling House on the same foundation. The first house was built in 1795. The old house was moved in 1883 to provide a temporary residence until this house could be completed. A service of dedication was held on Thanksgiving Day 1884. Since this time the house has served as the center of life for the Community. The building is six stories high and contains 48 rooms.

of our spiritual health and growth, of discipline when necessary, of settling the problems among us girls, and was in all ways our mother. But it was Sister Mabel who was responsible to Sister Mildred for all decisions concerning us, and was with us on a daily basis. It was Sister Mabel who made life fun for our group of girls. When she left the Community during the Second World War, it was devastating to the entire Community, but especially to our group of girls who had thought of her as one who would always be with us. Her leaving was a great personal loss to me, and I missed her terribly. Sister Mildred knew my feeling of loss and of betrayal, and allowed me to write to her occasionally. Young people were generally not encouraged to keep in touch with those who left. After a person had left the Community, they were not allowed to come to visit for a period of a year. Mabel came to visit us after a year. She eventually married and had three daughters. She and her family would come each summer to spend a week or more with the Community, who continued to care about her. I kept in touch with her until her death in 1990.

After I moved into the Dwelling House, many changes took place in my work. I began taking a two week stint in the kitchen along with three others. The kitchen work was set up so that the same people were not always doing the work. Four people, consisting of head cook, baker, vegetable girl, and sink girl worked for a period of two weeks, and then had a month off. In a short

Sister Mildred's teenagers. This shot was taken the first year I moved into the Dwelling House. I am the middle one in the first row. Sister Mabel, Sister Mildred's assistant, is the third from the left in the second row.

time, I discovered that I thoroughly enjoyed working with food, and doing food related work. I am not saying that I enjoyed the work of sink girl, with the huge amount of pots and large pans to clean up for the seventy plus people we were feeding at that time, but I did enjoy the camaraderie of the three people with whom I worked closely. All of the cleanup was not left to the sink girl; usually the cook and baker would help out with that chore. Sometimes the other girl in the kitchen would also help. Life in the Community kitchen was an enjoyable experience. I was fortunate in working with Sister Ethel and Sister Mabel much of the time, but there were times when the Sister who was cook took the title literally, and never helped with any of the other tasks.

Another change in my work took place when I moved into the Dwelling House. Sister Iona had been in charge of the hen and egg business for years, and Sister Elizabeth worked with her.

Kitchen Crew. Left to right—me (sink girl), Marjory (baker), Sister Mabel (head cook), Lucy (vegetable cook).

The younger girls in the Dwelling House took turns helping. Each of us had a morning each week in which it was our responsibility to gather the eggs. I was terrified the first time I had to do this. Many of the hens were protective and did not want to lose their eggs; they pecked at my hands when I tried to gather them. I decided to use a long stick to push the hens out of the way, but when this came to the attention of Sister Iona, she did not accept it well. Naturally, what I was doing disturbed the hens, and good egg production depended on their well-being. "Happy hens make good eggs," and the egg industry at that time was one of the better financial ventures at the Community.

It was decided that Lorraine and I could work together collecting the eggs. This meant that we both worked two mornings a week, but Lorraine was agreeable to this. With her help I had no problem gathering the eggs.

We also began doing more outside work. With war looming and talk of our country becoming involved, it was difficult to find summer help to work in the huge vegetable gardens. We teenagers became more involved in bringing the produce in to be canned for winter use. We usually did our garden work in the morning when it was cool. In the afternoons, we worked with Sister Elsie in the canning rooms. These were situated in the basement of the Sisters' Shop. Sister Elsie was a hard worker, and though there were times when the girls irritated her, she was a fair person most of the time. The hot and often tiresome work over the boiling arch kettles had its moments of fun under her supervision.

We gathered in the large room overlooking the plum orchard for our work. As we girls sat, we pared and cut up fruits and vegetables to be preserved in glass jars. We used the hot water bath method of canning. Sister Elsie kept the fires going, and prepared the syrups for the fruits. She filled the jars and placed them in the large kettle.

The older Sisters who were helping usually finished their work around 4:00 p.m., and Sister Elsie was left with us girls to finish the cooking and cleaning up. By 4:00, we were beginning to tire, and were eager to be finished. Sister Iona had a radio in her sewing room, and we had gotten into the habit of visiting her at 5:00 and listening to the soap opera, "Young Widow Brown." We were wholly addicted to the program.

Sister Elsie would listen to one after another of us make excuses as to why we couldn't work past 5:00. To her credit, she would often excuse us on a late day, but my older sister Katie would remain. Katie and Sister Elsie were good friends, and Katie had grown adept at the preserving trade. Katie was also Eldress Prudence's right hand when she was making mince meat.

Many aspects of the fancy work of the Sisters, and especially the poplar work, were usually done in the winter months. I thoroughly enjoyed weaving the poplar and became adept at it. All of the girls were expected to weave six inches of poplar each day except on the weekends. We could do this before school began at 8:30 in the morning, and if we didn't finish, we could finish after school at 4:00 p.m. With so many girls weaving, the looms were kept busy. Hundreds of poplar boxes of all sizes and designs were made each year, and this required hundreds of yards of woven poplar. In addition to the weaving, during peak times, we girls would often wire the strips. This was sewing the poplar onto a wire or sewing wire onto the poplar. We would do this vital work in the evenings. While we were working, Sister Mabel would read from a book of our choice, which made the time fly. At the end of the evening, we would have a good supply of strips for the next day's work. We did not help with any other aspect of making poplar ware.

Another project on which we worked as teenagers was

penwiper dolls. These little dolls with china heads were dressed in pleated skirts of felt, with a top formed by a crossed over ribbon. These were a popular item when ink pens were in vogue. When ball point pens came into use, these penwiper dolls went out of production.

I enjoyed dressing these dolls and did well making them. We also dressed larger dolls in long dimity dresses. When I come across one of these dolls, I remember those summer days with nostalgia. Today, these penwiper dolls, made by the Shaker girls, command a ridiculously high price from collectors.

At the time we were dressing the dolls, Sister Mildred was turning out aprons of all styles and designs for the Shaker Store and for the sales trips to the various resorts. Her sewing room was next to the room we used, and we would often help her with the aprons and pot holders.

When Sister Mildred's supply of pot holders and aprons was

View of the south end of the Shaker Store in 1942.

low, she would organize a sewing party for the evening. Each two girls shared a Shaker sewing desk and a sewing machine. Sister Mildred had the rare gift of turning a work event into a fun time. Funds were low at the Community during those days, which meant that there was little money for extra party foods. Sister Mildred, however, would create a festive meal by grinding up Spam or other luncheon meats, cutting bread into fancy shapes for sandwiches, and making Kool Aid. For a very special event, she would open some of the home made root beer. To our group of young people, who were only used to the meals served in the Community dining room, this change from the ordinary was a real treat. We crowded into the two sewing rooms, and had a great time.

When I was twelve and thirteen, I would sometimes become restless during these working hours, and begin to create a disturbance. I had the ability to create a disturbance by getting the other girls to fool around. When this happened, Sister Mildred would call from her sewing room and remind me that it was time to practice the piano. There were many times during those summer days that I left the sewing room to practice the piano. What an astute person Sister Mildred was!

Shortly after I moved into the Dwelling House, the teenagers, under Sister Mabel and Sister Mildred, were given the large room at the Children's House for a club room. This room, situated in the ell of the Children's House, was separate from the Children's quarters, and was a place where we could have privacy and an opportunity to do our own thing. In our room were a piano, a radio, and a gramophone. We were so happy to have a place of our own where we could be by ourselves, and we would spend the late afternoons and evenings there. Because it was unheated, we could use it only from spring through late autumn.

The north window of our club room looked over the Community clothes drying yard. During good weather, everyone hung clothes in the clothes yard. One learned quickly where to hang them. Although there were no outward signs, the older Sisters hung their clothes in certain squares, and the young people had the lines further away from the laundry. Unless there was a sudden shower and the clothes got wet, we were supposed to bring them in before dark. We were not to leave straggling lines of clothes hanging out.

The Sisters' retiring room looked out over the Children's House, and Sister Mildred was able to see most of what went on there. One day, we girls had become so caught up in a radio program that we completely forgot to take in the laundry. Around 7:00 that summer evening, the intercom rang; it was Sister Mildred reminding us to bring in the laundry. When the call came, I had the sudden idea of making things a bit exciting. I suggested that we fool Sister Mildred by going out the window to the clothes yard. She would not see us until we came in to the Sisters' Shop, and she would think we hadn't gone out. It was easy for each of us to drop out of the window. But we underestimated Sister Mildred. As we were all leaving the clothes yard to take our laundry into the Sisters' Shop, Sister Mildred appeared in the window from which we had exited.

"Oh, nay," spoke Sister Mildred. "Bring it in the way you went out!"

The window was high off the ground, and we were wearing our Shaker dresses, but one by one with arms filled with clothes, we made the effort to climb up and through that window. As each girl climbed, the girl waiting her turn, would help the one before her by pushing her in through the window.

Sister asked, "Whose idea was this?"

"Mine," I replied sheepishly,

"You will be the last one to climb in," Sister Mildred replied.

How humiliated I was, but how wise she was.

Chapter Eight

◆ ◆ ◆

Coming and Going

As a young girl living at the Shaker Community, I did not leave the Community very often. I left only for a doctor's or dentist's appointment. However, on occasion special trips were planned to take us into the world.

Sister Jennie enjoyed taking groups of girls to the State Capitol in Augusta, Maine. When it came my turn to go with a group, I was extremely excited. I had not been away from the Community on a pleasure trip since I arrived. We watched with excitement as the kitchen Sisters packed a picnic lunch for us. Our trip would last for the day and we would eat along the way. To make it even more impressive, the Community had just purchased a new station wagon and our group would be the first to use it.

The day which began with such exhilaration almost ended in disaster as we gathered around the new car and tried to decide where each girl would sit. It turned to chaos as eight little girls squabbled over who would sit where. All of a sudden Sister Jennie ordered us all out of the car. For a moment we thought we weren't going anywhere. Then she said to us, "If I'm going to keep my sanity, you are going to have to sit where I tell you to." Then she told us that we would play musical car seats. Every so often she would stop, and everyone would change seats. She would do this often enough so that we all would have an opportunity to sit in every seat. And this we did! When she stopped, we each scrambled for a different seat. What fun we had! This was the type of person Sister Jennie was. She understood how children could get out of control, and rather than be stern and dampen our spirits, she made a game which would make our trip even more special.

The day which seemed to be targeted with calamity continued that way. When we arrived at the State House, we discovered that there were many other groups of young people there for the same tour, and the place was packed. As we entered one of the halls, one of the younger girls in our group suddenly threw up all over the group directly in front of us. She was prone to car sickness, but she had not mentioned to anyone that she did not feel well. Then pandemonium broke out. The teachers tried to care for those who had been "hit" and there were many trips to the wash rooms.

This episode took up a large amount of our time, so we were in a hurry as we continued on our tour. I was walking directly behind Sister Jennie. As we were going down a flight of stairs packed with young people, I heard a great tearing noise. Sister Jennie, like most of the older Sisters, wore long dresses. I had stepped on the hem of her dress which meant that as she walked, the skirt was torn from the rest of her dress! I could have died of embarrassment! But Sister Jennie, in the rush of all the people on the steps, simply gathered up the torn section of her dress and continued on. Because she had made this trip to the State House before, and because she was a Shaker Trustee, she was a well-known person. One of the young women at the State House came to her rescue. She took Sister Jennie into her office and with needle and thread sewed the dress enough so it would stay together for the rest of the day. I was a long time living down that mishap. To this day, whenever I walk down a crowded stairway, I check to see if I am going to step on someone's clothing.

Even though we had our own wonderful cottage on Sabbathday Lake, we also had the opportunity to go the seashore for a day's outing. In addition, we usually took a trip to Old Orchard Beach and went on the rides there.

During this time, there was a good deal of visiting between Sabbathday Lake and Canterbury. It was not unusual for visitors from Canterbury to come and stay for a few days. Usually a day's visit did not include the children, but I remember one particular day when we were all summoned to the Dwelling House to meet a Sister from Hancock. Sister Frances Hall had especially asked to see the children. When she heard that my name was Frances, she wanted to meet me. Sister Frances Hall served as the Trustee of Hancock Shaker Village. When I saw this person, who shared my name, it was hard for me to realize that she was a Shaker of some

Sister Frances Hall of Hancock, Massachusetts.

standing. She was rather portly, had beautifully coifed hair, was wearing a silk dress with a large floral print, and wore a string of pearls. She simply did not look like the Shakers which I knew. When I mentioned this to Sister Mary later, she told me that it was not what people wore that made them Shakers. I accepted this until a few days later when I heard some of the Sisters in the ironing room talking about the way Sister Frances Hall was dressed.

Another visitor to the Children's House was Eldress Emma from Canterbury. Before she arrived, Sister Mary had drilled us on how we were to behave with her. We were instructed to be on our very best behavior, but also to be natural, which was a difficult order to fulfill. Eldress Emma was a formal, dignified, and almost haughty-appearing person. She arrived, and the visit was going well. Then there was a lull in the conversation, and little Glennis looked up at Eldress Emma with the sweetest smile and asked, "Can you take out your teeth?"

Without the least bit of discomfort, Eldress Emma smiled back and asked, "Can you?" At this point, all the girls began pulling on their teeth. This was not quite what Sister Mary had hoped for.

Sunday afternoon was the time when Community friends and relatives came for a visit of an hour or two. One visitor that I remember well was Jane Ricker, who was married to J. B. Ricker, one of the founders of the prestigious Poland Spring House. The Rickers were well respected people in the area. Eldress Prudence told me that in the earlier years, the Rickers would come to the Shaker Eldress for Confession. She said there was a close spiritual bond between the Shaker community and the people who owned the Poland Spring complex and resort.

During my first year with the Shakers, the Millers, who ran a gift shop at the Poland Spring House, brought their daughter Betty to board at the Community. Betty and I became close friends, and it was difficult for me when Betty went home to the Poland Spring House on Saturday mornings. She usually arrived back late on Sunday afternoons. Once in a while, her parents would ask for and receive permission to take me and another Shaker child for a ride and ice cream. Those were special times indeed.

Eldress Emma B. King of Canterbury, New Hampshire. The photograph was taken on the front steps of the Children's House. Eldress Emma is surrounded by five of our girls.

The Millers were summer residents only. When it was time for school to begin, they would move to Florida, where they operated a gift shop at another resort. It may not have been the ideal way for a little girl to grow up, but to me at that time, it seemed like a wonderful way to live. As the time for Betty to leave for Florida drew close, we were unhappy; it was difficult for us to be separated. Betty told me she was going to ask her folks to adopt me, but of course they didn't. It was several days after she left before my life got back on a normal course.

During the last year I lived at the Children's House, a woman by the name of Dorothy Poole came to live with the Community. We were told that she would be "trying the life" as she was interested in becoming a Shaker. She must have had a good home, because one day a moving van brought a load of furniture from her home in Brockton, Massachusetts. She was given a room on the third floor of the Dwelling House, the northwest room directly over Eldress Prudence's sitting room. Dorothy took an immediate liking to the children. She would invite us to her room on Sunday afternoons which resulted in quite a bit of activity over Eldress Prudence's room. This turned out to be a real problem, since Dorothy was deaf and did not realize we were making so much noise

Although the children and young people were loved and cared for, the policy was that children should be seen and not heard. Dorothy, however, did not believe in this concept. This may have been the reason for her short stay with the Community. In no time at all, she began working in the kitchen as a cook. Here, she continued to show favoritism to us. Because the children and young people loved chocolate, she served chocolate bread pudding for dessert instead of the regular plain bread pudding. I remember watching and being amused when during meals, she would serve the children's table first, passing over the head table where the

Eldress sat. I remember having the feeling that she was deliberately doing this, but I never knew why. This did not go over well, and after a few months, Dorothy and her lovely furniture went back to Massachusetts. We children felt sad and missed our champion. Of course I never heard from her again, but I wondered if perhaps too much was expected of her, and if, given time and understanding, she might have stayed. A couple of the middle aged Sisters resented her "high handed way." I do know that one of them could not eat chocolate.

Chapter Nine

∽ ∽ ∽

At the Lake

The days that I am writing about were not affluent times at Sabbathday Lake. On the contrary, there was little money for luxuries even at a time when things were not costly. However, because of an extraordinary happening, we had a wonderful cottage at the lake.

It was the custom during good weather to take a walk to Shaker Hill after the noon meal was cleaned up and before the afternoon activities began. Occasionally, the usual time was not appropriate, and the walk would be slated for later in the afternoon. We girls always looked forward to this part of our daily routine. We loved exploring Shaker Hill, where there were many old ruins and foundations, as well as a few houses. This outing included anyone who cared to go and had permission to do so. Children from the Children's House and the teenagers went along with either Sister Mabel, our favorite, or Sister Olive, our not-so-favorite. Sometimes, they both went with us, as did some of the younger Sisters, as well.

On one particular day, we had gone just beyond the school house, when one of the girls shouted that she had found some money. Naturally, we all went to see what she had found. There she stood with a handful of bills. Before we got over the shock of her find, several other girls began finding money as well. The money was scattered over a short distance between the school house and the cemetery. As soon as we were sure we had found all there was, we hurried back to the house. Our interest in going to Shaker Hill had vanished.

Our find created an enormous amount of excitement at the Community. Sister Jennie, as Trustee, took the money and put it safely away. She immediately got in touch with the authorities and reported our find. For several days it was advertised, but there was no response from anyone. There was a great deal of speculation in the Community as to where the money had come from. I remember the final thought was that perhaps someone had been drunk and lost it, or that it might have been stolen, and someone had to get rid of it quickly.

Personally, I thought it had come straight from heaven, because in Sunday School, we had just had the story of the Israelites wandering in the desert, and the manna coming down from heaven.

After a period of time, when no claim had been made on the money, the Shaker Community was allowed to keep it. I have no idea how much money there was, but it was more than most of us girls had ever seen before. It was decided to use the money to build a cottage for the young people on Sabbathday Lake. What a wonderful idea this was to us! Before this, whenever we went swimming, we had to change into our bathing suits in the woods, with some of the girls being "lookouts." Now, we were going to have our own cottage!

Sister Jennie, along with the Elders and Trustees, had commissioned Otis Campbell to build the cottage. Work began on June 7, 1938. It was finished by the 23rd of June and painted on the 27th. What a wonderful place it was! Not only did we have a cottage with a screened-in porch, but there was a glider on the porch. There were changing rooms and a built-in table which formed a window when it was put in place.

The area around the cottage and leading to the beach had been cleared, and there were rope swings hanging from two of the largest trees. There was the loveliest little park cleared from what had been deep woods, and beach chairs had been purchased. One could not help but wonder what sort of fortune had been found.

We named our cottage, "Camp Jennie," and some of our happiest days growing up at Shaker Village took place there. Today, in spite of much vandalism and abuse, part of the little cottage still stands.

Several times during the summer months, a group of us would go to the Trues' cottage on Sabbathday Lake. The group included the girls and young people, as well as some of the Sisters. We would go to spend the day with this family, who had been friends of the Community for years.

A group down at "Camp Jennie" our cottage on Sabbathday Lake.

The large truck, loaded with picnic baskets, bathing suits, and towels, would take us to our cottage at the Lake. We would gather on the beach which is directly across from True's Point. The truck would leave, and we would wave a signal to the Trues who were waiting on the other side. Then two large boats would fly across the lake to pick up the people and supplies. It always took several trips to bring over all the people and supplies. When we arrived, we would spend the day swimming, playing on the beach, and doing all those things which one does on a outing at the beach. As darkness fell, we would load into the boats at Trues' Point and return to our beach, where the truck would be waiting to drive us back to the Village.

This was also an opportunity to see other people from outside the Community. The True family rented several cottages during the summer, and more than one interesting encounter developed from these visits. To this day the friendship continues as Margaret True Racette, who was a girl when I was, still operates True's Point, and we occasionally meet around town.

Chapter Ten

◦ ◦ ◦

Celebrations and Celebrating at Shaker Village

Preparing oneself spiritually for the Christmas Season, being ready to receive the Christ, has been a part of Shaker theology and an important aspect of Shakerism. As the Season of Advent approached, we became aware that an important event, known as Fast Day, was about to take place. Whenever I heard any reference to it from an older person, it was always in a serious tone of voice. There was a feeling about it that made even the youngest of the children realize that it was a sober event.

Sister Mary told us that it was a time when every person in the Community, from the Eldress to the youngest child, would have Confession. Confession was also spoken of as "opening one's mind." Each person would go to the one in charge for Confession. We children went to Sister Mary; the older girls to Sister Mildred; the Sisters from Alfred to Sister Harriett; the older Sabbathday Lake Sisters to Eldress Prudence; Sister Jennie would hear the young Sisters who were not from Alfred, and would also be the confessor for Eldress Prudence; and Eldress Prudence would be Sister Jennie's confessor. I must admit that we young people did a lot of wondering about what Sister Mary would confess.

Fast Day was exactly what the name implies. Cooking and

eating were minimized even more than on ordinary Sundays. There was an atmosphere of something hushed, not frightening but sobering. When the Family was large, the Fast Day was divided into two Sundays. During these two Sundays, the Sunday Meeting was different. Brother Delmer would read the Shaker Church Covenant and rules as part of the service. This was not the most interesting Meeting for young children, but we were expected to sit through it, and we did.

Christmas was a meaningful and festive time for the children and young people at Shaker Village. The Community had a huge tree which reached to the ceiling of the Winter Chapel. The girls and the boys each had a smaller tree in their living quarters. The festivities were held on Christmas Eve. A pageant was followed by gift giving. It was an exciting night. Any gifts we may have received through the mail from family or friends were placed under the tree. Besides these, there were gifts from the Community members

Christmas Pageant, 1940.

and friends of the Community. Many of these friends were generous with the children and young people. Eldress Prudence had a friend who always allowed each child to make a list of five items that she would get for us. We were encouraged to keep the gifts simple and inexpensive, but still, five gifts coming from one person was something special.

The small tree at the Children's House was another part of Christmas. Right after breakfast on Christmas morning, we would open the gifts under this tree. There were always wonderful games, puzzles and books for the girls to enjoy.

Shaker Meeting was and is still held at 10:00 a.m. on Christmas Day, followed by a delicious dinner. The afternoon was free to enjoy the new gifts and each other. Christmas was always observed in the same way as the Sabbath, so we did not go outside with new sleds.

We had plenty of opportunity for sledding in the days that followed. One of our favorite slopes for sledding was the long field and hill leading from the orchard to Route 26. Fifty years ago, there was not as much traffic there as there is today, and so it was a safe place to slide. We did not do much skiing until we were in our early teens.

Halloween was a fun time. Often there was a large party organized by the older teens and middle aged Sisters. The party was held in the ironing room which was decorated for the occasion, and most people wore costumes. A harvest supper was prepared, and family friends from the world would be invited to come. It was quite the evening with all types of games and contests taking place. We children were invited to this festive party, but we had to leave before the evening was over. We felt we had missed out on a lot of the fun.

Birthdays were always noticed in some way at Shaker Village. It was ironic that I shared the same birthday as Sister Mary. It was not usual for a child to have a birthday cake while I was at the Children's House. It wasn't until I was under Sister Mildred's care that birthday cakes became a reality. On our birthdays we received gifts and were given the day off. Having the day of my birthday off was a two-edged sword. It made me feel special, but since my birthday came in March, usually it wasn't possible to be outdoors, and time hung heavy on my hands. Thankfully, I enjoyed reading, and would spend my special day reading books that I loved. I still have a few special little gifts which Eldress Prudence gave me for my birthday, and our collection has some which I felt belonged there.

Because of Eldress Prudence's hospitality and gregariousness, there was a great deal of entertaining going on. Many famous people spent time at the Poland Spring resort or at the Centennial

Children and older girls in their Halloween costumes, circa 1941. I am the Red Cross nurse (back row extreme right).

Spring House, situated a mile south of the Village. Many of them found their way to Shaker Village through their friendship with Eldress Prudence.

The Cooper family owned and maintained the hotel called the Centennial Spring House. Without a doubt, they were the closest friends of the Shaker family, and were an extension of the family. Eldress Prudence, Sister Jennie and Sister Mildred were especially close friends with them. Several times a year, they would come to the Community for Sisters' birthdays. Mr. Cooper drove the neighborhood students to the Shaker School and would always stop to say hello. During the summer and autumn months their hotel was filled with guests, and there was much visiting back and forth.

There was always a special evening of music when the quartet from the Centennial Spring House came to the Village to give a concert. The quartet consisted of Frank Cooper, Jr. and three college boys who worked as waiters. All of the young people were invited to the Meeting Room to be part of this wonderful evening. I remember how impressed I was one time when they announced they were singing a song dedicated to Eldress Prudence. The song, "Little Old Lady, Time for Tea," seemed so appropriate for this little lady. To my impressionable mind, it seemed like the most wonderful thing anyone could do.

For many years the older teens and younger Sisters in the Community had an orchestra. I can remember first and second violins, a cello, a trombone, trumpets, drums and cymbals as well as a piano. Many of the musicians in the group took music lessons from a teacher in Lewiston.. The Shaker Orchestra became quite professional, and often gave concerts at the Village. Sometimes it joined with other community orchestras in the area to present a combined concert.

Chapter Eleven

Sister Mildred

Eldress Prudence asked Sister Mildred to take over the care of the young people who would be coming from the Children's House to the Dwelling House to begin life within the inner circle of the Community. She would be taking over the work of Sister Iona and Eldress Harriett who were growing older. Eldress Harriett, who moved here in 1931 from Alfred, had been responsible since then for the young people who moved here with her; Sister Iona had been caring for the young people from Sabbathday Lake. It was an urgent time for choosing a Mother and mentor, and Eldress Prudence felt that Sister Mildred would best fill the role. At the time she was asked, Sister Mildred was recovering from a serious illness, and she requested more time before she took on this added responsibility.

Because of this, the girls who would be moving out of the Children's House had to remain there for a period of time. This caused overcrowding, with three girls living in the space where two had been before. Needy children were continually asking for entrance into the Community, so there were always new ones coming in.

Fortunately, Eldress Prudence had the wisdom to wait for Sister Mildred, or my life story would have been greatly altered.

Knowing her limitations in health, Sister Mildred agreed to accept the position with the understanding that Sister Mabel would be her assistant with the girls. Having Sister Mabel as her assistant gave Sister Mildred the few extra moments of rest that would not have been possible otherwise. It was as nearly perfect an arrangement as could have been planned. Sister Mabel never took advantage of being more than a friend in a casual relationship. She and Sister Mildred worked well together and were good and trusted friends.

Earlier, I talked about my move to the Dwelling House and my little room. Some of the defiance which I had experienced in the Children's House must still have been with me, in spite of the fact that I was now where I wanted to be. I remember the first night in my little room, Sister Mildred came by to see if I was all settled and comfortable. As she was leaving, she asked, "Have you said your prayers?"

I responded, "Nay."

"Of course, you are going to say them," Sister Mildred replied.

I had every intention of saying them, for prayer had become important to me, but I saw my chance to do a little testing and answered, "Oh, I don't know. I may or may not."

Instead of becoming upset or surprised, Sister Mildred completely disarmed me by asking, "Would you like to say them with me?"

We knelt together by my bed, and that started a tradition which lasted throughout our lives. Unless one or the other of us was away from the Community, we had our prayers together for the next fifty years.

It did not take long for all of us to get together and discuss the difference in our lives since moving to the Dwelling House. The subject of Confession came up, or as the Shakers referred to it, "the opening of the mind." This bothered most of the young

Sister Mildred Barker as I first knew her.

people more than it did me. Perhaps this was because of my Catholic background. Sister Mildred took the responsibility for our spiritual upbringing seriously and met with us every two weeks on Sunday morning. On Saturday evening, she would let the girls she would be meeting with on Sunday know. We girls would get together to see who had been chosen.

When we went to Sister Mildred for Confession, she always sat in a Shaker rocker with a straight Shaker chair next to her for the lucky or unlucky person. Sister was a beautiful woman in her 40's and 50's; she presented a lovely picture in her navy blue Shaker dress and Shaker cap. The response she usually received from us was, "I haven't done anything wrong." But Sister wanted to keep the doors of communication open between her and her young people.

Although she was a warm, loving person, she was a strict disciplinarian when she had to be. If one's behavior warranted it, she would deprive that person of something which meant a lot. Her theory was that if we were going to act like children, we would be treated like children. Being sent to one's room was often used as a form of punishment. During my first year in the Dwelling House, I spent a great deal of time in my room.

Because there were many older people living in the Dwelling House, we were expected to be in our own rooms with a minimum of noise by 8:30 at night. This was difficult but necessary because Eldress Prudence, who slept one floor below us, went to bed early and did not look favorably on any disturbance. We were, however, allowed to read for a longer time. Breakfast was at 6:30, and those working in the kitchen were up by 5:30.

Many a night, I would sneak from my room and go down to the end of the hall where Lorraine and the other girls were. I would only make it as far as the door of their room when Sister Mildred would appear and send me back to my room. She slept across the hall from the girls' room, and I often wondered how she ever got enough sleep. She was aware of every unusual sound which came from her flock.

Lorraine suffered from asthma and would make weekly trips to Lewiston to visit an allergist. Often the time of her appointments would come at the same time as dinner. When this happened, Lorraine and those who were with her would be given lunch money and they would buy their lunch. But when Sister Mildred was one of the people, *she was never hungry.* She used her lunch money to buy candy for her girls.

This was a time when money was scarce. If there were to be Christmas gifts, they had to be hand-made. Sister was a beautiful seamstress, and one Christmas, she made all ten of her girls housecoats in their favorite colors. Another year, she managed to find a fine soft muslin and made each of us a dozen handkerchiefs. When we would ask her what she would like for Christmas, it was always something which was within our reach. She would love to have an embroidered holder for opening the stove in her sewing room, or a pair of pillow cases. She would find a pair of plain pillow cases that needed some fancy work. Her bureau drawer is still filled with hand-made scarves and doilies for her room. She treasured the exquisite work which some of the older girls did. On one special occasion, when we needed a gift that would be meaningful to her, she suggested that we all do a piece together. Each of us added our work, and with ten different hands working, this turned out to be a masterpiece. The work ranged from the very best to a pitiful example of French knots.

Under Sister Mildred's care, we experienced our first birthday parties, complete with cakes. She was a wonderful cook and had a recipe for a special chocolate cake that we all knew would appear on our birthdays. Our birthdays were full of expectation, since we never knew when the cake would appear. Because of the large number of people living in the Community, our birthday parties were separate from the meals. Often they were held in our sewing room with all of the young people present. Fancy sandwiches with fillings, that we would not normally have, would be served along with potato chips, Kool Aid and cake.

Sister Mildred came to the Alfred Community at the age of seven. She did not see or hear from her mother for years. After she assumed the caretaker role at Sabbathday Lake, an aunt, who had long been looking for her, discovered where she was. This aunt was crippled and unable to travel to see Sister Mildred, but she did write to her weekly and would send her a couple of dollars when she wrote. Sister Mildred used this money for the girls' parties.

Sister knew how to make each person feel special when that was important. She had a special touch in our times of illness. As soon as we were well enough to eat, she would fix a tray with delightful little dishes kept for that purpose. Her creamed toast with a dropped egg on it was a treat that almost made a cold worthwhile.

In the dining room, Sister Mildred sat at the table with her girls. Although there was little, if any, conversation during meals, she taught us table manners. Because she had been a finicky eater as a child, she was understanding about our dislike of certain foods. All she asked was that we try a teaspoonful of the food. She would not tolerate any arguments at the table. As a group of teenagers, we sometimes had arguments. We learned to argue in whispers and with our body movements. When this happened, she would leave the table. Her leaving the table was the worst thing that could happen, to our way of thinking.

Sister was also concerned for our physical well-being. She took the responsibility of guiding us through puberty and into the teenage years with the same wisdom and understanding that she showed in other areas. During my teenage years, Eldress Emma was a frequent visitor to our Community. The Canterbury Village had not had young people living with them for some time, and in the pre-war era, they probably had no idea of how to deal with teenagers.

One time when Eldress Emma came to visit Sister Mildred, she was eager to share a book with us called, *Nancy's Thirteenth Birthday*. This book probably had not been read by any young person for years, but because Eldress Emma wanted us to "learn from it," Sister Mildred expected us to comply. We read it as a group, and became terribly out of hand and silly over the Victorian aspect of preparing a young person for puberty. Even though Sister Mildred tried to conceal it, she too was amused. Sister Mildred had the rare gift of being able to communicate well with her young people. When one of her girls made the decision to leave the Community, she was not allowed to go into the world as a naive and innocent person. Sister did not want her girls falling prey to the dangers that could befall a young person who had led a sheltered life.

She was able to communicate with each of us according to our personal needs. During my last year at the Shaker School, I became attracted to a boy from the world. His family was new in this area, and going to a country school was as new for him as it had been for me. I had more opportunity than the other Shaker students to share a friendship with him because I was assisting the teacher. In the school room I was not confined to my desk; I was at school before the rest of the Shaker students, and I stayed later.

Sometimes he would wait for his father to pick him up, and I would wait with him under the old mulberry tree. I took every opportunity to be around him and the feeling was mutual. We "goofed off" in the typical way teenagers did.

I did not say anything to Sister Mildred about this part of

my school life, but of course she found out. She could see the school yard from her sewing room and bedroom, and there were always the watchful eyes of the Sisters in the Ministry's Shop, as well. Sister Mildred's amazing understanding and wisdom manifested itself again. She began to casually talk about this boy, and she let me know she knew more that I thought she did. Instead of telling me I was a Shaker girl and my life did not allow for teenage romance, she simply reminded me that my situation was unique. She explained to me that since I was an assistant to the teacher at school, I was a role model to the other students, and my behavior had to be better than what was expected of others. She never told me that I must stop associating with him, but each day after school, she would ask about him and give me the opportunity to talk about the situation. This made it open and an enjoyable time for me. Sister Mildred never forgot that we were typical young teenagers with the normal tendencies of teens everywhere.

In spite of Sister's frail health in the late 1930's, it was amazing how well she held up during those years when she cared for so many teenagers. Most winters, she had a bout of pneumonia or was threatened by it, but she bounced back after a few weeks and seemed to thrive on her responsibility.

Although Sister's first responsibility was to the spiritual and physical well-being of the teenagers, she lived the Shaker motto, "Hands to work and hearts to God." She not only lived these words, but she also made work a memorable and fun time for us. She personally made hundreds of aprons for the Shaker Store and the sales trips. She made thousands of pot holders, and supervised our making and dressing of the penwiper dolls and china head dolls. She made the trip to the Summit Springs Hotel, a few miles from the Poland Spring Resort, which drew vacationers from all over the country to this lovely rural spot. Twice a week, Sister would tell us that she and another Sister would be gone for the day on sales trips. We would be left under the supervision of Sister Mabel. On these trips, wealthy women would order sweaters and coats to be knit by Sister Mildred. In all of her work, she involved her girls, teaching us to sew and knit. In spite of all she was doing, she worked with Sister Jennie making candy, jellies and pickles, which were sold. It is a rare gift to make work fun and Sister had that gift.

Everyone who knew Sister Mildred knew of her love for music and singing, especially the Shaker spirituals. These Shaker songs soon became a part of our lives. On Friday evenings it was common for Sister to gather us in the waiting room where we would learn Shaker songs. She had the foresight to teach us these Shaker songs so that they would be carried on to another generation. She never realized at the time that her singing would be recorded for future generations. To her, the Shaker songs were something she loved and wanted kept alive.

Sister Mildred loved opera, and each Saturday afternoon, she would listen to the opera broadcast on the radio as she knit or sewed. We all understood that this was her time, and we did not disturb her.

Sister Mildred believed that idle hands were the devil's workshop, and she kept our time well filled. Every other Friday evening was the "Girls Improvement Club" meeting. Sister Mildred organized this club, which continued our education by a special emphasis on literary work, study, and concentration. We were assigned subjects on which to write, wrote and learned poetry, and had musical presentations, with piano and other instruments. Being young people, we lost little time in attempting to minimize the importance of this club. We dubbed it "GIC" in the same derogatory sense in which young people today use the term "geek." Actually, having expressed our cynicism, we did enjoy the club and learned from it as well. We not only learned to write, but we learned to present our work properly. In addition to all of the other teens and Sister Mabel who were present, Sister Mildred always invited a different Sister to participate. This kept us on our toes in spite of our pretended indifference. We did want to present our work well.

Club night, as those Fridays were called, meant dress up, for no sloppy dress or hair, and no misbehavior were allowed. We were encouraged not only to present well written compositions, but also to help in assigning subjects to others. This did not always work well, because sometimes our peers would choose an unimportant work for us. This did not go over well, and we would use it as a way of having fun.

One time Lucy, a girl a few years older, and I were to memorize a poem and say it in unison. We learned the poem, but in the process changed some of the words so it sounded ridiculous. At the time of our presentation, we planned to say the correct words. It is not easy for two giggly teenagers to recite a poem in unison. We began on cue, but as we remembered the words we had changed, we went into a fit of giggles. Sister Mildred gave us a chance to sit down and compose ourselves, but our second effort was no better than our first. All we could do was laugh, and by now our silliness had spread to all the other girls. Our guests that evening were Eldress Harriett and Sister Eva. Poor Sister Mildred realized that we were not going to be able to control ourselves, and she excused us and sent us to our rooms for the rest of the evening. It was quite a disgrace, and it was an evening when refreshments were served following the program!

In retrospect, the Girls Improvement Club was an exceptional learning experience. To this day, I do not give a paper without hoping that I do credit to Sister Mildred, who gave so much of herself to teach those of us growing up Shaker.

Many of the girls, with whom I grew up in the Shaker way, continued through the years to come back and see Sister Mildred. They remembered her on special days, including Mother's Day. Some people may feel that Shaker Sisters are unfulfilled because they do not have children, but this was not the case with Sister Mildred. I, like many others, bonded with Sister Mildred, and no other person could have made my life happier than she did. I wish all young people could experience the happy years which I had under Sister Mildred. In spite of the hardships, her life as caretaker of the girls was a rewarding one. Sister Mildred loved her girls and in making the commitment to them, fulfilled the words of the Psalmist: "He maketh the barren woman to be a joyful mother of children."

Sister Mildred with her group of teenagers, 1940. This photograph was taken after Meeting and the girls are posed in their new Shaker dresses.

Chapter Twelve

❧ ❧ ❧

The War Years

World War II greatly affected life at Shaker Village. The younger Sisters, teenagers and older girls began to do much more of the outdoor work than before. It was difficult to find anyone to work on the farm. The defense plants and other war related industries took all the people who had not joined the military.

My brother Bill left the Community to join the Army, and my brother Herbert was also serving in the Armed Forces. An unexpected bonus of the war time was the substantial improvement in my grades and those of my little sister Ruth: when Bill left to join the Army, he began sending us a dollar every time we got an A on our report cards. Soon, my older brother Herbert began doing the same thing. This was not only an encouragement for us to do well in school, but it reminded us that we had not been left and forsaken. All of a sudden we felt well off financially. Never in all the time we had been living at Shaker Village did we have so much spending money.

Although the Shakers have always been and still are pacifists, when young men known to the Community became a part of the war effort, much correspondence went on with them. Just before America entered the war, Sister Jennie called us to her office and told us that my sister and I must write at least once a week to Bill and Herbert. This in itself was astonishing, since there had always been a minimum of correspondence between the young people and the world. Two letters a month to parents were all that were normally allowed.

We continued to work out-of-doors throughout the fall, and returned to the work waiting to be done in the sewing rooms. It was nearing the Christmas Season, and Eldress Prudence would be looking for the special items which we always made for her to take to her sale at the Columbia Hotel.

Now that Americans were becoming involved, we were encouraged to listen to the news nightly. Our club room was closed for the winter, and our favorite gathering place was Sister Mabel's room. There we would read and listen to her radio. One Sunday afternoon, just before supper, we were relaxing and listening to music, when the program was interrupted with a special newscast. The Japanese had bombed Pearl Harbor. The United States had at last been brought into the Second World War. It was December 7, 1941, a day that would change our lives in many ways. President Roosevelt referred to it as "a day that would live in infamy." For the Sabbathday Lake, Maine, Shakers, as well as for every American, it was the beginning of a whole new way of life. It was a time of food and gas rationing, and a time of heightened expectancy and fear as we began to live in a world at war.

For many of us, it was the first experience of being at war. Even now, I remember well the tension that took over, as people were glued to radios, anxious to hear the latest report of the war. It was a world so different from that to which we were accustomed.

The first weeks and months of 1942 saw many changes taking place. In February, Eastern War Time went into effect as we set the clocks ahead one hour. The Trustees purchased bolts of black material, and the Sisters under the tutelage of Sister Iona made blackout curtains for the Dwelling House. In case of air raids, the lower hall of the Dwelling House, and the smaller cellars leading from it, were to be the air raid shelters. Everyone was to leave the houses they were in and gather in the lower hall of the Dwelling House. The first air raid drill for this area began at 9:00 p.m. on April 28, 1942 and lasted until 9:30 p.m. It was preceded by the ringing of the big bell atop the Dwelling House.

In April of 1942, a major event took place at the Community when it was decided that young girls working on the farm could wear slacks. There had been much discussion over this issue. Certainly, climbing apple trees and being on ladders had much to do with this decision. But it was not an easy decision to come to for many of the older members. For the first time, Shaker dress was giving way to worldly clothes. A compromise was reached when it was decided that the young people could wear slacks, but instead of worldly tops, well used Shaker dresses would be cut off at the waist, and the waist along with the cape would serve as a top. However, in a matter of months, the makeshift tops had given way to blouses or sweaters.

As was the custom, the purchases made by the Community Trustee were made in large lots. Large numbers of slacks were purchased in the sizes the young girls wore, and given to the individual girls. I was an extremely thin teenager and this was no doubt taken into account when I was given my first pair of slacks— in bright orange!

The introduction of slacks was a traumatic time for me. When I was working in the kitchen, I would not have my work finished when the truck left for the orchard and fields, so when my kitchen work was done, I would have to walk up the school house lane. When I passed the Ministry's Shop where Eldress Harriett, Sister Olive, and Sister Eliza worked, I would see them pointing at me and wagging their fingers in shame.

A group of us in our new slacks, 1942. Note that we are still wearing the upper portion of our Shaker dresses with the slacks.

It was difficult for them to accept the change. Later, however, when Sister Olive began to help with the outside work, she, too, wore slacks, and the attention focused on me and the bright orange dissipated. After the first purchase, most of the slacks and jeans were blue denim or another dark color.

May of 1942 saw the planting of enormous war gardens. String beans were for some reason a priority, and the Community planted one full acre of beans. The *Church Journal* records that on July 1st, 30 bushels of beans were picked; on the 4th, 64 bushels; on the 7th, 23 bushels; and on the 15th, 16 bushels. This made a total of 133 bushels of string beans that were picked for the war effort in July.

My recollection of the string bean harvest was the sight of

every able bodied person, who could be spared from the regular routine, gathering at the south end of the garden. There the entire field, which extended to the Merrill's farm, was planted in string beans. It was a time of fun for those of us who were young. At noontime we would find ourselves under the apple trees for a substantial picnic lunch, which was prepared by the Sisters who were not able to pick beans. With everyone joining in to make it as easy as possible, the work took on a festive atmosphere.

In September of 1942, the shortage of farm workers had become so serious that the Town of New Gloucester closed schools in order to allow school children to bring in the farm produce. There were no men available. They had gone to war or war related work.

At the beginning of 1942, the Community had decided to change the time of breakfast from 6:30 a.m. to 7:30 a.m., but this did not seem to work well. It was finally decided to have breakfast at 7:00 a.m., except for Sundays, when it was at 7:30 a.m. In November, the breakfast hour was changed again to 7:30 a.m. in order to save on fuel and lights. It remains at 7:30 a.m. today.

The days of working out-of-doors were the happiest of my young life. We were healthier than we had ever been. Although we were doing hard physical work, we were relaxed in our work. At our noon break, we ate picnic style. With the freedom of slacks, there was clowning around at noon. Once in a while, Brother Delmer would become annoyed with us, and tell us sternly, "If you do not behave, I will have to let you go."

Of course, we knew he could not let us go; we were all the help he had. Most of the time he found this new freedom with the young people as delightful as we did. Because of our good relationship with him, Brother Delmer dubbed Ruth Rupert and me "The Heavenly Twins."

There were acres of potatoes planted. When it came time for

the potato harvest, Brother Delmer asked if we could also do that work. The work involved picking up potatoes which the potato harvester had dug. Sister Mildred spoke to us about it, and we were enthusiastic. Sister Mildred, being the astute person she was, and knowing that Christmas was coming, told Brother Delmer, "Yea, the girls can do the potato harvest, but it is only fair that you pay them a little, because it is hard work."

"I will give them five cents a bushel, " replied Brother Delmer.

"Seven cents a bushel will be more acceptable," responded Sister Mildred.

A rather lengthy and heated argument followed, but in the end Sister Mildred won out. Again, a bit of history was made; for the first time, people living in the Community were working for wages. I believe the way this was handled so smoothly was by acknowledging that the money was a gift to encourage us, and not wages. Who would work for seven cents a bushel and call it wages??

Group picking up potatoes. Sister Olive is in the foreground waving the "V" for victory sign to the photographer.

Because of gas rationing, little travel was done by car. A bus went by the Village going to and from Portland and points north, so those who needed to go to Portland went by bus.

One day, Lorraine and I were allowed to go to Portland on the bus with Sister Genie, who had an appointment there. Sister Genie did not want us bothering her for the rest of the day, so we assured her that we were able to take care of ourselves. After looking around the city, we hurried to the theater for the afternoon performance of "For Whom the Bell Tolls," which starred Ingrid Bergman. We kept this a secret for a long time, and made up little white lies to cover our trail. I am not sure what we expected to see, but, whatever it was, it went over our heads. What was intended to be a really daring escapade on our part, was not as daring as we had thought.

When the season of outdoor work ended, with the apples and potatoes all safely harvested, we turned our attention to the late fall and winter work. By this time, my work in the kitchen had changed. No longer was I sink girl and vegetable girl; I had graduated to baker which meant I would be making bread, pastries and many of the cookies. The head cook did the desserts which were not baked foods. I now held a responsible place in the kitchen crew which consisted of Sister Mabel as head cook, myself as baker, and a new girl who had recently come to the Community as sink girl and vegetable girl.

The year of 1942 was, on the whole, a different but happy time for those of us who were teenagers. We had a large chart hung in the kitchen to assist us with rationing. Because this Community had always been frugal in purchasing food, things did not change much due to rationing. Because there were so many people in the Family, we had a large number of food stamps. Thanks to the foresight of Eldress Prudence, staples such as sugar, one of the most rationed foods, were in stock. There were barrels of sugar, flour, and other foods in the storeroom.

By the time summer was here, gas rationing went into effect. This did not affect the teenagers because we seldom went anywhere by car. It did, however, have an adverse effect on the sales trips to the ocean side resorts, mountains, and other places. As a result, the Community began to feel the financial strain. This was also the beginning of the demise of the well-liked poplar ware. It became impossible to obtain the kid for binding the poplar ware boxes. Other materials became almost unobtainable because many manufacturers had turned to the defense effort.

The young people still went to the lake during the autumn months to enjoy walks to Loon Point. All of a sudden, it seemed that a frenzy of war efforts swept the country, the world and finally penetrated our little Village with a greater impact than anyone could have predicted. No longer was there such a thing as a quiet

All loaded up to go up harvesting, 1942. Hiram May, our hired man is the driver.

day. Many of our neighbors were traveling to Portland for defense work, which brought large increases in their salaries. There was a new friend each day going to "join up." Because we are situated between Brunswick, a major air base, and Portland, a major seaport, we began to experience more of the turmoil which wars create. Planes were constantly flying over the Village; Route 26, which goes through Shaker Village, became a major route for transporting the military. Some days unbroken lines of military vehicles rolled through Shaker Village from early morning until darkness fell. Because of the large number of vehicles in a convoy, they moved very slowly. All of this was a great attraction to the young people.

The Sisters, who normally spent many hours at the Ministry's Shop, did not attempt to cross the highway. The old horse block was still standing just north of the Dwelling House, and every free moment we could muster was spent sitting there watching the convoys pass. Sister Mildred tried to keep us away from this attraction, but it was late summer, and when we were not at work, it was impossible to keep us indoors. Even many of the older members watched from the windows so there was no way the young people could be denied the excitement of being part of what was happening.

One day, when most of the teenagers and younger Sisters were outside, a truck filled with soldiers came right up to the entrance of the walkway, and the soldiers began tossing slips of paper with addresses on them, asking that we write to them. One or two of the bolder teenagers ran to the truck and brought a handful of addresses back to us.

Earlier, I mentioned the fervor with which Sister Jennie and Eldress Prudence encouraged me and my sister to write to our brothers, and for some reason they allowed several of the younger Sisters to write to Servicemen. This was supposed to aid the war effort, but in the end it proved to be a grave mistake resulting in several Sisters leaving the Community. It resulted in a restlessness which could be called a "casualty of the war." Ironically, nothing lasting ever came from those war-time friendships.

The Poland Spring and Summit Spring Hotels were not busy, because people no longer had gas for traveling to stay at the hotels. Wealthy people now turned their attention to the "war effort" — entertaining Servicemen and doing all types of volunteer work termed "patriotic." Because the Sisters seldom went to the hotels to sell their goods, they tried to increase the sales at the Shaker Store, which had also been affected by gas rationing. But Sister Iona still accompanied Eldress Prudence to the old Columbia Hotel in Portland for the three-day sale, and we spent more time with Sister Mildred in the sewing room making special items to enhance the Christmas sales.

The number of young people and children continued to grow with the admission of a family of three to the Children's House and a family of four to the Dwelling House. Community life continued to be full, busy and, for the most part, happy. However, there was a major change during the next year when eight people left the Community. Four were taken by family members, but the other four were three teenagers and Sister Mabel. She was a Sister on whom such dependence and love were centered that it was a great shock to the entire Community. Two of the older girls were natural sisters and they both joined the WAVES. The other was my older sister, Katie. I had realized for some time that she probably would not make a Shaker, but it was still a painful experience to have her leave. She and Eldress Prudence had been good friends. She was a strong, healthy girl who was never sick, so she was depended on for many things. Earlier, Eldress Prudence had told her that if she stayed and became a Shaker, she would appoint her as a Second Eldress when the present one passed away or became infirm. But this did not sway Katie's resolve to leave. One has to wonder what might have developed had she remained here at Shaker Village?? In the years I had been here, she truly became a big sister to me, and it was difficult to have her go.

But Sister Mabel's leaving was much more difficult. She had become an important part of my daily life. I worked with her in the Community kitchen, and she was our companion on most of our pleasure jaunts. I could not imagine life at Shaker Village without her. I can only imagine what Sister Mildred must have felt: her assistant in caring for the girls and her dearest friend had left. Sister Mildred must have experienced a feeling of betrayal. Sister Mabel had been a covenanted Sister for eight years, and I am sure there were high hopes for her leadership in the future because of her talents.

With four people leaving the Community within two months, many adjustments had to be made. I found myself working as baker under Sister Elizabeth. She never cared for cooking. As a young person, she had been under the care of Sister Iona who was an excellent seamstress. Sister Elizabeth became a proficient seamstress and knitter, but she never did well with cooking. After a long time of working at the task, and not caring for it, she asked if I would be willing to change places with her if the Eldress approved. At this time, I was having a problem with my hands; they swelled and I had to wear rubber gloves. I was all for the change if it was approved. It was, and I became head cook with Sister Elizabeth as baker. Two girls ready to move into the Dwelling House worked with us. It was a far cry from the time I spent with Sister Mabel, but we made it work and I learned a lot. Sister Mildred had kept her cooking talents hidden, but at a time when I needed a bit of encouragement and help, she was there to give it.

During these years, we still had dairy cows and made our own butter. Sister Ethel was in charge of the dairy as well as taking a turn as cook. During the times we were both off kitchen duty, I would help in the dairy. This was not one of my favorite things, because I heartily disliked the smell of butter and cheese.

The longer the war went on, the more it affected our lives. Daily, we were aware of the struggles going on all over the world. We listened to daily newscasts, and General Eisenhower and General Patton became household names. D-Day, June 6, 1944, dispelled any sense of well being which may have remained at Shaker Village. It brought the war closer in a way that we did not think it could. Our lives at Shaker Village had seemed so safe and secure that we were not prepared for the loss of lives and the injuries resulting when the invasion of Normandy took place after months of planning by the Allied Commanders. On June 6th, the Community was called to a special prayer meeting for the country and its Armed Forces.

We still heard from my brother Bill, but letters from Herbert became nonexistent. One evening I was going upstairs to my room, and as I passed by Eldress Prudence's room with its open door, she called for me to come in. Sister Della had just taken a supper tray to her. She was well into her 80's and had a light supper in her room at night. She spoke to me, "Frances, Herbert was just here."

I looked at her, not knowing what to think or say. I wondered if she was beginning to wander a bit mentally, but she was as firm as anything as she continued. "As Della came up the stairs, she saw Herbert taking the stairs two at a time on his way to my room. Then I saw him." That was all she said but it had a ring of truth to it, and knowing from past experience her closeness to the Spirit world, I did not question, but I did not give it too much thought.

We were well into the summer; July was half over and still the war continued. We lived our lives as normally as possible. My little sister Ruth had moved into the Dwelling House a few months earlier, and she had become quite mature, helping Sister Mary care for the small children. The Children's House was filled to capacity, and one of the girls who had come at age five, had grown enough to help with the smaller ones. So Ruth was brought in to be with Sister Mildred's girls. Although she had been happy at the Children's House, I'm sure she was glad to be with us, and I was happy to have her close by.

About a week after Eldress Prudence told me about Herbert, we were preparing to go to the lake for the day to escape the heat. We had packed a picnic dinner so we would not have to be back to the Village until early evening. Around noontime, Sister Jennie summoned Ruth and me to her office to tell us that word had come that Herbert had died. He had been in the invasion of Normandy, and after a month of being in the thick of things, had answered a volunteer request to put a German machine gun nest out of commission. This had prevented the Americans from gaining a strategic hill. His mission was referred to as a "suicide mission," and was successful, but he was badly wounded on July 10th and died from his wounds on July 12th. He was wounded on the day that Eldress Prudence saw him come into her room.

It was the strangest day for us. Ruth and I did not know what to do. Because of the lack of family ties, Herbert had told people that if he died in Europe, he would not expect to be brought back to the United States, and so there were no funeral preparations. This was the first encounter with death that Ruth and I had since coming to Shaker Village. We were in a quandary— should we go to the lake for a day of fun or should we stay home and come to grips with the death of our big brother?

The entire Community felt a real sense of loss, because everyone who had known him cared for him. All of a sudden the war had reached Shaker Village. Sister Mildred talked to us at length and reminded us of how Herbert loved the out-of-doors, especially the area around Sabbathday Lake. He had often told us that he found it easier to worship God in a forest than in any man-made church. We did go to the lake where we spent the day.

A few days later, letters from Herbert came to both of us—letters he had written before the mission. In the years he was living here, long before we came, he had known Elder William. He told us in his last letter that for days he had been strongly reminded of a song written by Elder William. The song: "I see the light before me, 'tis guiding me still farther on, along my heavenly journey, unto my future home." What better eulogy could we have had.

With fall work needing to be accomplished and the lack of workers continuing, again, we took on the potato harvest. However, we did not work in the orchard because Brother Delmer for the first time brought a group of Jamaicans to do that work. During the apple season, about twenty of these people worked on the harvest. They were able to do it more quickly than we were able to.

One day as we worked in the potato fields, a large bomber plane flew overhead. It flew unusually low, which made us wonder if the crew were checking on us. We realized something was wrong when it went down in the woods, exploded and burned. This caused a lot of excitement in the Community, but we were not able to discover what had happened to the men on board. Had anyone survived? We did not realize how classified and hushed up this incident was until the next day. We were working in the potato field again and wondering what it was all about, when we looked up and saw a military jeep driving across the field toward us. An impressive officer stepped out of the jeep and walked toward us. Two other military men remained in the jeep. The officer asked us numerous questions, and we asked him a few, but got no answers. Then he said to us, "If you want to be good Americans and help the war effort, you will refrain from discussing with other

Brother Delmer Wilson, 1942. Brother Delmer would get into his truck and drive up through his apple orchard nearly every day. Here he was discovered enjoying a lunch in his beloved orchard.

people what you have seen." He made us feel that we were involved in some way with an important mission.

Through the late afternoon and into the night, we heard all sorts of activity around the Village, but we never heard any more about what happened. There was never any mention of it in the newspapers or on the radio. During this time it seemed that our lives, as we had known them before the war, would never be the same again. Too much had happened in the world and in our lives as we were growing up in Shaker Village.

Another teacher from the world had come to the Shaker School in 1942. She was a nice young woman and was popular. She had her own personal problems because her fiancee was serving somewhere overseas, and she was constantly in dread of something happening to him. From Monday through Friday, she lived in the Trustees' Office, and became a real friend to the older teenagers. She owned a car and, when gas was available, would take some of us for a brief outing. However, after two years she became seriously

The harvesting crew enjoying a treat in the orchard, 1942.

ill, and Sister Mary, who had been tutored for this type of emergency, began to teach at Shaker School.

As a result, more of the younger girls came into the care of Sister Mildred. Again, we had a full roster of younger teens. As younger girls came into the house, Sister Mildred enlisted my help in some of the everyday activities with them. Lorraine and I were still close friends, and a girl from New York joined us.

There is nothing more true than the fact that young people are resilient, and bounce back from traumatic experiences. All of us, some more than others, had gone through some difficult times, but still life went on and we were, on the whole, a happy lot. The new girls coming from the world, who were in their early teens, came directly to the Dwelling House rather than spend any time at the Children's House. With Sister Mary teaching, the younger children were cared for by her assistant, a teenager, and Sister Gertrude Soule.

In May of 1945 the war in Europe ended. After the invasion of Normandy, we knew it would only be a matter of time before the fighting in Europe would come to an end. On May 18th, the Shaker Community joined all the churches in a day of prayer to give thanks for the end of the war. In August Japan surrendered, and the war in the Pacific was finally at an end. Special prayer services of thanksgiving were held, and soon much of the food rationing came to an end.

Chapter Thirteen

~o~ ~o~ ~o~

I Become a Shaker

Once the war years were over, life everywhere began to settle into a more normal routine. Our life at Shaker Village began to have more structure than during the war years. No longer did we have to shortchange some duties and tasks in order to fill in where the Brothers or hired men usually worked. Life within a Community does tend to follow a routine, and while it was good to return to our routine, I found I missed the outdoor work which had been so satisfying.

I have always loved the wind; loved to walk on a windy day and pit my strength against the wind as it blows and tears at my garments. For several years I had been, for the most part, a carefree young person, letting the "wind" blow me where it would. It was not always easy accepting the changes that occurred during that short time of my life: losing loved ones through a parting of ways or death. It is never easy to face and accept change when one is young and believes that no matter what happens, like Scarlet in *Gone with the Wind*, "When I get through this tomorrow will be good; it will all go away." I think at that age, when so many changes had taken place, I tried to put it out of my mind; to hide my head in the sand, thinking that if I ignored it, it wasn't too bad.

As I approached my sixteenth birthday, Sister Mildred had a

long talk with me telling me that life had been turbulent and exciting for the young people. But now that Lorraine and I were the only two left from the ten girls who were with her when I came under her care, it was time to give serious thought to what I intended to do with my life. She had noticed over the last couple of years that I seemed to be leaning toward becoming a Shaker.

Two months after the war ended, my sister Ruth left the Community. She had been an important part of my life for as long as I could remember. I was now the only one from my personal family still with the Shakers.

Over the years I had seen so many young people leave. For the children whose parents took them, it was easily understood. But it was more traumatic for the Community, and especially Sister Mildred, to have so many young people choose to go to the world when she had put so much of herself into their care. I can only imagine how disappointing, hurtful and hopeless it must have seemed. Yet, to this day, it amazes me how the Shakers, especially those who cared for young people, accepted the choices they made without recrimination. I mentioned this to Sister Mildred, and she replied that the young people who left were under the care of the Shakers until they came of age, did not ask for it, and they had no choice. So now they were entitled to make a choice they felt would bring them happiness.

I felt a great pity for the Shakers at this time and decided that I would be the one to remain. Those who knew me as a child and as a young teenager, would never in their wildest dreams have expected that out of the ten, I would be the one to remain with the Community. Lorraine shared these feelings in a different way. She, too, felt sorrow that so many had left during the eight or nine years of our living together, but she made it no secret that she was not meant to make, nor did she want to make a life-long commitment. To her credit, however, she did stay on long after

Sister Frances.

she might have left, in order to help the Community with the younger teenagers. She left the Community two years after she signed the Covenant.

Surely, life goes in cycles, and after almost ten years here, my life had come full-circle. I was now the oldest girl and helped with the younger girls. Again, there were ten girls living in the Dwelling House doing the same things I had done; going through the experiences I had experienced; and rebelling in the ways I had rebelled. It was easy for me to relate to them.

It was time now for my life to go in a straight line; to focus more on maturing, not only physically, but more important, spiritually. While it was a good thing to have feelings of wanting to give back to the Community something of what it had given to me; good to want to make up for the loss of others; good even to believe that I was finally leaving the defiance and rebelliousness behind; one cannot base a life of commitment to God and the Shaker life on these things. There must be a fuller understanding of what commitment means. Although the study of Shakerism and Mother Ann's teachings had been a part of our education while growing up Shaker, Sister Mildred and I began to have intensive talks and study on what it was truly all about; what it would mean; what I would be expected to give up if I made the decision to become a Shaker.

There could not have been a better teacher. Sister Mildred, without a doubt, lived the Shaker life more completely than anyone I had ever known. One day as I was near the end of my teenage years, Sister Mildred and I were with Eldress Prudence as she was cutting out aprons in the Sisters' Shop. Eldress Prudence said to Sister Mildred, "You have done very well with our Frances."

Sister Mildred replied, "Nay, Frances has done very well with Frances."

"She will make quite a woman if she puts her mind to it,"

responded Eldress Prudence.

I hope I have not disappointed her. On a day in May, I was summoned to Brother Delmer's room and in his and Sister Mildred's presence signed the Shaker Covenant. Surely God does write straight with crooked lines. My growing up Shaker days had ended, but my real growing days had just begun.

Sister Frances and Sister Mildred.

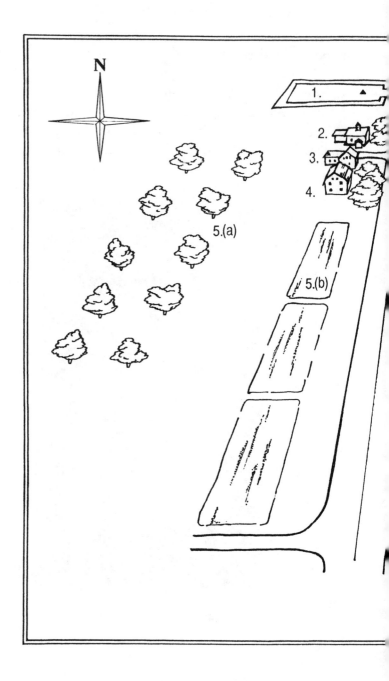

1.

2.

3.

4.

5.(a)

5.(b)

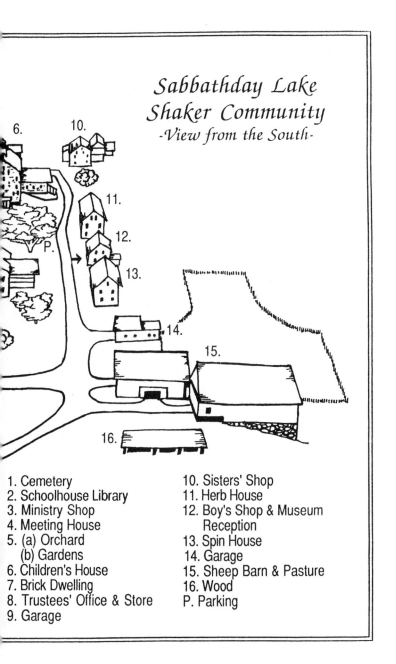

Sabbathday Lake
Shaker Community
-View from the South-

1. Cemetery
2. Schoolhouse Library
3. Ministry Shop
4. Meeting House
5. (a) Orchard
   (b) Gardens
6. Children's House
7. Brick Dwelling
8. Trustees' Office & Store
9. Garage
10. Sisters' Shop
11. Herb House
12. Boy's Shop & Museum
    Reception
13. Spin House
14. Garage
15. Sheep Barn & Pasture
16. Wood
P. Parking